"I had left Courcelle[...]26 officers. Now, before m[...] For 17 days they hadn't had a cup of hot co[...] of hot food. They hadn't taken off their shoes. They hadn't had a chance to wash their faces. Even drinking water had been scarce for days. Their only rest had been on bare ground. For the last four days they had even been without packs. . . . They had driven trained German veterans out of fortified positions by frontal attack; had walked into the fiercest kind of woods fighting in France; had taken nearly twice their own number in German prisoners, and captured more than 50 machine guns and half a dozen trench mortars. They had made a record never surpassed in the war."

COLONEL WISE/the 4th Marine Brigade

DO YOU WANT TO LIVE FOREVER!

When the German offensive struck, the French General in command was in Paris with a lady of pleasure. Without warning, 15 German divisions broke through the Allied lines and drove to the Marne, pausing only to re-group before pushing on to take Paris. The only troops left who could possibly stop them were the Americans who had just recently arrived in France and who had never seen battle. After hurried consultations with General "Black Jack" Pershing, it was decided to commit a brigade of U. S. Marines. What happened afterward is one of the most glorious pages in Marine history, and one of the most thrilling and exciting stories to come out of the war.

Do You Want To Live Forever!

by Richard Suskind

BANTAM BOOKS · TORONTO · NEW YORK · LONDON

DO YOU WANT TO LIVE FOREVER!
A Bantam Book / published November 1964

Library of Congress Catalog Card Number: 64-25022

All rights reserved.
Copyright © 1964 by Richard Suskind.
Published simultaneously in the United
States and Canada.

FOR GINETTE

"The grass soon grows over a grave."
—GEORGE SANTAYANA, *Soliloquies in England*

AUTHOR'S NOTE

I wish to express my gratitude to Mrs. Martha Holler and Miss Edith Midgette of the Department of Defense, and to Major Robert F. Prentiss of the U.S. Army, for their help in making this book possible; to Mr. Robert Loomis for his constructive criticism of certain passages; and most especially to Mr. Charles Kirchman for his patience in guiding me day after day through the stacks of the National Archives.

CHAPTER 1

SHORTLY after eleven a.m. on Decoration Day, May 30, 1918, a black De Dion-Bouton limousine pulled into the courtyard of a big slate-roofed château on the outskirts of Chaumont, France, swung around a line of parked motorcycles and staff cars, and came to a stop before the entrance. Without waiting for the chauffeur to open the door for him, General Henri Philippe Pétain, chief of staff of the French Army, climbed out and, with surprising agility for a man of sixty-two, ran up the short flight of steps leading to the main hall. A sign over the door read: Headquarters, American Expeditionary Force. The doorway was flanked by sentries wearing white puttees and cartridge belts. Pétain returned their salute, repeated the gesture with the colonel who came hurrying to meet him, and was immediately shown up to General Pershing's office on the second floor.

The two generals conferred for nearly an hour. In the corridor outside, where an authority-inspired hush prevailed, passing officers and secretaries could hear the murmur of their voices coming through the door—Pétain's melodious baritone, redolent of St. Cyr and French salon society, the interpreter's neutral tones, and Pershing's weak, reedy tenor, incongruous in so big a man, which still held traces of his native Missouri twang. "The temptation to pause and eavesdrop was overwhelming," one of these passing officers wrote in a letter to his brother. "We all knew that something big was in the wind, otherwise Pétain wouldn't have come in person. But the fishy eye of the guard at the door persuaded me to hurry on about my business."

1

Something big indeed was in the wind. Not since the first months of the war had the Allies' situation been so precarious, or the prospect of victory so remote. Once again, for the second time in four years, the Germans had smashed through the French defenses and were on the Marne less than forty miles from Paris. Soissons had been taken, Reims seemed certain to be next, and sixty-five thousand prisoners as well as enormous quantities of guns, ammunition, and other matériel had fallen into the enemy's hands. The roads leading west from the battleground were clogged with fleeing soldiers and civilian refugees, hampering French efforts to send up reinforcements. The panic had spread to Paris—now, like London and Berlin, a city of women, old men, maimed veterans, and children—and every day saw the railroad stations thronged with people cramming themselves aboard trains that would carry them to safety. Impelled by bad news from the front and by the nerve-racking bombardment of the three giant railroad guns known as "Big Berthas," which intermittently lobbed shells into the city from seventy-five miles away, nearly a million people had already fled the capital. The government itself was packed and ready to move to Bordeaux, and in the Chamber of Deputies it was touch and go whether the faction headed by Joseph Caillaux, a former finance minister and an outspoken pacifist, would not take power and seek an immediate treaty with the Germans. The main reason this had not yet happened was that Caillaux's strongest supporter, General Maurice Sarrail, was not in Paris to help him carry out this coup. The general was pinned down with his army in Salonika, Greece, in what the Germans jokingly referred to as "our largest internment camp."

Inside the office, pacing with short, nervous strides before the open window, Pétain reviewed the situation in detail, emphasizing its gravity, before he came to the point of his visit. The window gave onto a large formal park behind the château, and sunlight slanting through a pair of chestnut trees cast a leafy pattern of light and shadow across his slim elegant figure, resplendent in a horizon-blue uniform with the Médaille Militaire and the Croix de Guerre, France's highest decorations, pinned

2

to the tunic. The sardonic, pessimistic, highly intelligent Pétain—acclaimed a hero the year before for having put down the revolt of the French Army; condemned as a traitor twenty-seven years later for having collaborated with the Nazis—had spent the past four days in his headquarters near Compiègne, working around the clock to halt the retreat, and was obviously very tired. "He ran on nerves alone during the crisis of May and June," one of his aides wrote. "His thin aristocratic face was haggard and his eyes red and swollen. He slept no more than three or four hours a night." Whatever his other faults or virtues, Pétain had a deep and genuine concern for the plight of the men in the trenches.

It was extremely doubtful, he explained to Pershing, if France could survive the loss of Paris. The capital was not only the spiritual heart of the nation, the symbol of *La France Héroïque,* it was also an important industrial center and the focal point of all the major railroad systems. The country was exhausted both morally and physically after four years of the holocaust that had consumed an entire generation of her sons; the loss of Paris could easily be the decisive blow. General Foch had committed almost all the remaining French reserves to the sector under attack, holding back only the minimum forces necessary for a last-ditch defense of the city. These reinforcements, however, had not yet succeeded in stemming the enemy advance, and any further German successes, even local ones, could have far-reaching effects. That was why, Pétain concluded, he had come to Chaumont personally to ask General Pershing to send American troops to the danger point.

This request was not as simple as it may appear. It was in fact the crux of an extremely delicate and touchy issue: the disposition of American troops. And even though Pershing had anticipated it, had talked it over with his aides earlier that morning and decided, reluctantly, that he had no choice but to comply, he still reflected long and carefully before committing himself.

There was an air of confidence and authority about this dour-looking fifty-eight-year-old man with the weathered, regular features and close-clipped mustache who was seated rigidly upright behind the desk. General John

J. Pershing was not brilliant, or popular, or a magnetic leader of men. There was nothing of the showman or the charlatan about him. Indeed, despite his colorful nickname "Black Jack" (it did not refer, originally, to his toughness; it had been given to him, in a spirit of mockery, when he commanded Negro troops in the Philippines), he was perhaps the most colorless commander America ever put into the field. His troops called him "a typical brass hat," the correspondents "a cold arrogant fish," and even his friends and admirers could find no more flattering adjectives to describe him than "discreet," "thoughtful," and "dispassionate." He was a plodder, an unimaginative man who plugged stubbornly away at an objective until he attained it. It is a brutal fact that, if his father-in-law had not been Senator Francis Warren of Wyoming, chairman of the Senate Military Affairs Committee, he would very likely have ended an undistinguished career as a retired colonel or, at best, a brigadier general. With the Senator's support, however, he merely had to make no serious mistakes to be assured of rapid promotion. He made no such mistakes, served competently, if without distinction, in the western United States, the Philippines, and Mexico, and in May, 1917, was appointed commander-in-chief of the A.E.F.

As is sometimes the case with nepotic appointments of this sort, he proved to be a good man for the job. He was a fine organizer, was shrewd enough to choose competent men as his aides, and he had two qualities in particular that were of inestimable value: tenacity and patience. It was these qualities that had seen him through a terrible personal crisis in 1915, when his wife and three daughters were burned to death in the fire that destroyed their home in San Francisco. It was these qualities that had kept him chasing Pancho Villa, the revolutionary and bandit, through the dusty hills of Mexico for eleven fruitless months—a campaign, incidentally, that brought the name "Black Jack" Pershing constantly before the public and paved the way for his appointment as commander in chief. And it was these qualities that enabled him to cope with the obstacles placed in his path by the French and British leaders. For the simple, startling fact was: the Allies did not want an American Army in Europe!

Ever since the United States had entered the war in April, 1917, the French and British had done everything they could to prevent the formation of an American Army. They looked upon the United States as a sort of gigantic supply depot from which they could draw endless amounts of cannon fodder to replenish their own depleted armies. David Lloyd George, the British prime minister, wanted the Americans fed singly into his divisions; Georges Clemenceau, the French Premier, was willing to accept them by companies and battalions. Neither of them wanted an American Army, for its presence on the battlefield would automatically give the United States a voice at the conference table when the war was over and the spoils divided, and they sharply distrusted President Wilson's idealistic approach to world affairs.

It maddened the prime ministers to see shipload after shipload of strong healthy young men debark and be sent to training camps for formation into divisions, while they themselves were reduced to drafting mental defectives and essential workers in war industries, and sending men back to the trenches who had been wounded, in some cases three and four times. It did not seem to matter to them that these healthy young Americans had received only the most rudimentary training in the States, working with wooden rifles, stovepipe mortars, and manuals that had not been revised since the Civil War; that "not one man in ten knew a machine gun from a cream separator and many had yet to learn the first fundamentals of military life." This did not signify, the Allied leaders said. Stick a rifle in their hands, show them how to pull the trigger, and put them under "experienced" French and British officers (i.e., those who had been lucky enough to survive the "sausage grinder"): they could fight and die as well as the next man. After all, their ambassadors and special envoys in Washington argued, why build up an American Army? The French and British had been engaged in the greatest war in history for nearly four years; they had the organization, the staff

5

and field officers, and above all the experience. Why not let them continue to run the show? Besides, the United States had not had an army worthy of the name since Appomattox, had fought nothing since then but the comic-opera campaigns in Central America, China, and the Philippines, and would waste many crucial months building a force capable of meeting the Kaiser's gray-clad veterans on equal terms.

These arguments impressed certain congressmen and senators, especially those from the isolationist Middle-Western states, and they even caused Secretary of War Newton D. Baker to waver. But they left Pershing and, what was more important, President Wilson, unmoved. The United States was a first-rate power; therefore it should have a first-rate army. That was the sum of Wilson's reasoning, and his written orders to Pershing, defining the commander in chief's discretionary powers, specified that "the forces of the United States are a separate and distinct component of the combined forces, the identity of which must be preserved. . . . The decision as to when your command or any part of it is ready for action is confided to you, and you will exercise full discretion in determining the manner of co-operation." Pershing meant to carry them out to the letter.

It required all his tenacity and patience to do so, for not only the French and the British, but the Germans as well, conspired against him.

As the winter of 1917-18 drew to a close, Quartermaster-General Erich Ludendorff, the guiding genius of the German general staff and Field Marshal von Hindenburg's right-hand man, prepared one last massive effort to win the war before the arriving Americans tipped the balance irrevocably against him. His chances of success seemed good. Serbia and Roumania were prostrate; Italy had suffered the disastrous defeat at Caporetto, in which she lost two hundred thousand men and all heart for further offensive action, and was now more of a hindrance than a help to the Allies; and Russia was out of the war, dismembered by the Treaty of Brest-Litovsk and far too involved with her great social experiment to resume the conflict on behalf of the Tsar's capitalist allies. Furthermore, the general staff estimated that the United States would be unable to deliver more than fifteen untrained divisions to Europe before the spring of 1918—too little, Ludendorff calculated, and too late to save the Allies.

While the Western Front remained in a frozen stalemate and the opposing armies apathetically regarded one another across the churned-up horror of No Man's Land, Ludendorff pressed every available train and truck into service to transfer troops from the defunct Russian Front to France and Belgium. All winter, at the rate of ten divisions a month, the battle-hardened veterans flowed across the snowy plains of Hungary and Poland, through Germany and into France. By early March some three hundred thousand men had made the journey, and for the first time in the war the Germans had numerical superiority on the Western Front. Ludendorff planned to use this superiority to split the Allied armies, drive the British into the Channel, then turn and finish off the French. On March 21, as if to celebrate the first day of spring, he launched a great drive towards Amiens, the vital junction of the central and northern railway systems and the meeting point of the French and British armies.

"Operation Michael," as this initial assault was named, very nearly succeeded. The British Fifth Army was all but destroyed by the onslaught. Before he was relieved of his command for incompetence, defending General Sir Hubert Gough threw in labor battalions, railway troops, cooks, clerks, shoemakers, and tailors; and the French rushed reinforcements from as far east as the Vosges. These desperate measures succeeded in halting the Germans, but only after they had driven a wedge thirty-five miles deep and sixty miles wide into the Allied lines. Although Field Marshal von Hindenburg had hoped for more, he was not dissatisfied with the results of the attack. "Man's work always proceeds piecemeal," he remarked philosophically. For the Allies the near-disaster had one beneficial effect: after four years of squabbling with the French and jealously guarding their prerogatives, the British finally realized the neces-

7

sity for a unified command, and accepted, reluctantly and with many reservations, General Ferdinand Foch as Supreme Allied Commander.

This great offensive forced Pershing to realize that an American Army would not serve much purpose if the war was lost while it was taking shape, and on March 22, in response to the Allies' anguished appeals for help, he called on General Foch and told him: "The American people would hold it a great honor for our troops were they engaged in the present battle. There is at this moment no other question than that of fighting. Infantry, artillery, aviation, all that we have are yours to dispose of as you will."

Foch was delighted. Not only would the American troops and matériel stave off defeat, but by assigning them to the French and British, Pershing had inevitably delayed the formation of the American Army, and this was precisely the aim of the Allied policy-makers. "The American troops will fight side by side with the British and French troops," the Supreme Commander declared in an official communiqué, "and the Star-Spangled Banner will float beside the French and English flags in the plains of Picardy." But Pershing swiftly disillusioned him. He was willing to help the Allies, yes, but he had no intention of commanding a replacement depot for them. When the speeches and mutual declarations of esteem had been made, when it came down to hard facts, he would only allow American troops to replace French ones in quiet sectors of the front, releasing the poilus for more active duty elsewhere.

This arrangement did not satisfy either the French or the British, who wanted nothing less than huge transfusions of manpower with no strings attached. Lloyd George was especially indignant, or so one would assume from what he said, for the volatile, brilliant Welshman was a master of rhetoric and could change moods with astonishing rapidity and conviction when it suited his purposes. "If the war is lost," he warned Pershing, "it would be lost honorably by France and England, as they would have expended their last for us in the struggle. But that for America to lose the war without having put into it more than Belgium would not be in compatability with

8

American pride and American traditions." And F[...]
an effort to intimidate the American commander in[...]
spoke ominously of "hoping to hold out until Augus[...]

But Pershing, as stubborn as one of his Miss⸱ari
mules, was not to be intimidated. "America declared
war independently of the Allies," he reminded Foch,
"and she must face it as soon as possible with a powerful army. The morale of our soldiers depends upon their
fighting under our own flag. America is anxious to know
where her army is." (It is interesting, though of no great
significance in the present context, to note that the only
American troops to fight the war under a foreign flag
were four regiments of Negro infantry. Despite their
repeated requests to be allowed to rejoin the A.E.F.,
these troops were held in French divisions scattered from
Alsace to Champagne. America, it seems, was not so
anxious to know where they were.)

Lloyd George and Clemenceau alternately pleaded
with and cajoled Pershing, and their ambassadors in Washington suggested, as boldly as they dared, that Wilson
replace him with a general more amenable to the "dic-
tates of common sense," but to no avail. Supported by
the President, Pershing stuck to his guns with a tenacity
bordering on fanaticism. He meant to put an integral
American Army on the battlefield if he had to skirt professional disaster to do so.

On April 9 Ludendorff attacked again, this time further
north against the British and Portuguese forces near
Ypres. The brunt of the attack was directed against the
Portuguese, and the Germans quickly broke through.
Three days later the situation was so critical that Field
Marshal Sir Douglas Haig, that indomitable dispenser of
other men's lives, issued a special order to the Army
that read in part: "There is no other course open to us
but to fight it out. Every position must be held to the
last man; there must be no retirement. With our backs
to the wall, and believing in the justice of our cause,
each one of us must fight on to the end. The safety of
our homes and the freedom of mankind depend alike
upon the conduct of each one of us at this critical moment."

It was not these beautifully balanced phrases, how-

9

ever, that halted the Germans short of their objectives. After four years in that "ditch of blood which ran between the borders of Switzerland and the North Sea," the average Tommy was immune to appeals to his patriotism. He not only did not believe in the justice of his cause, but doubted whether such a cause had ever existed; and he cared nothing at all for the "freedom of mankind"—whatever that might mean. He was, as Robert Graves, Siegfried Sassoon, Edmund Blunden, and other British chroniclers of the First World War have pointed out, concerned only with survival, with getting a "cushy" wound that would carry him back to a comfortable hospital bed in "Blighty." No, it was not empty phrases but flesh and blood in the form of more French reinforcements that stopped the Germans from driving the British into the sea.

On April 23, a few days after this attack had been halted, Pershing made a further slight concession to the Allies. To speed the transfer of American troops to Europe, even though they were half-trained and poorly equipped, he signed an agreement with Lloyd George to transport them in British ships. Lloyd George first tried to use his fleet as a weapon of extortion, offering to bring the troops to Europe if Pershing would assign them to British divisions. But Pershing told him bluntly, "If you have ships to bring over recruits to your armies, you have them to bring American divisions to the American Army," and the Prime Minister unwillingly conceded the point.

This agreement was the subject of a sharp exchange at the fifth session of the Supreme War Council, held on May 2 in the Grand Trianon Château in Versailles. The atmosphere at the meeting was thick with the mutual envy and mistrust with which the French and British regarded each other, especially as concerned their rapacious intentions towards the Americans. Clemenceau opened the session by accusing the British and Americans of plotting behind his back to deprive him of American troops. With characteristic theatricality, he rose slowly to his feet, leaned his paunch against the edge of the huge conference table, brushed his thick white mustache with the back of his hand, and addressed Viscount Alfred Milner, Lloyd George's envoy to the Council.

"The military representatives," Clemenceau began, "express the opinion . . . that only infantry and machine gunners should be sent to France for the present. Since then the agreement between Lord Milner and General Pershing, signed at London on April 24, 1918, has intervened. This agreement makes a change. It had been understood that America would send 120,000 men per month which the French and British armies would share equally. Under the Milner-Pershing agreement, it appears none are to go to France. The French have not been consulted. We might suppose in compensation that the American troops arriving in June would be given to France."

This statement bristled with so many misconceptions and outright lies that Lord Milner hardly knew how to reply. Finally, after a long astonished pause, he said: "Monsieur Clemenceau has intimated that there was something mysterious about the London Agreement. He appears to believe that the Agreement was signed in reversal of the Supreme War Council's decision. Besides, Monsieur Clemenceau seems to be under the impression that half of the American troops were to go to France and the other half to Britain. I do not recollect any such decision. All that General Pershing and I have urged is that infantry and machine-gun units should be sent to France. I do not know that anything has been said regarding their allotment on arrival in France."

Then Pershing, seated beside his old friend General Tasker Bliss, the permanent American representative to the Council, stood up with an angry frown. "In making the agreement with Lord Milner," he said, "I had in mind bringing troops as rapidly as possible to meet the existing situation. Lord Milner is quite correct in stating that there was no agreement as to the allocation of American troops, either to the British or to the French armies. There is no agreement between my government and anybody else that a single American soldier shall be sent to either the British or the French. There *is* in existence an agreement between Mr. Lloyd George and myself that six divisions should be brought to France."

11

While the French and British quarreled like starving dogs over an especially meaty bone (for the tone of their arguments suggests no more savory a simile), the Germans continued their preparations for the next blow. "I was aware," Ludendorff was to write later, "that the difficulty of deciding the war before American support became effective grew more and more. Nevertheless I adhered to my original intention, knowing that only our initiative and the best use of available time could bring us success."

With the attack in the north temporarily stalled, Ludendorff decided upon a diversion against the French line in the Chemin des Dames sector between Soissons and Reims. This should, he calculated, draw the French reserves south once more and permit him to consolidate his gains on the Amiens and Ypres fronts, then to resume his drive against the British. An attack in this sector had several things to recommend it: it would appear to threaten Paris, always the most sensitive point with the French; it would offer Crown Prince Rupprecht of Bavaria, field marshal of the Northern Armies, a chance to redeem his failure at the Ypres salient the year before; and most favorable of all, German intelligence had discovered that this sector, naturally fortified by four rows of hills that had proved impregnable to attack in 1917, was defended by shattered divisions, most of them half-strength or less, which had been sent there from the débâcle in the north to "rest and recuperate."

The French High Command knew that another blow was soon to fall. But where? Foch was convinced it would come in the north, towards Amiens once more. Some of his advisers suggested the moribund front in Alsace as a likely target; others thought the attack would come in the Vosges, now that the line there had been weakened by draining off troops to meet the German assault in the north. There was even a rumor, discounted by all but the most panic-prone of Foch's staff, that the Germans were preparing to violate Swiss neutrality and flank the entire French line. Perhaps the only sector in the 350-mile front that was not seriously considered was the Chemin des Dames. Foch thought an attack here so unlikely that he completely neglected even routine intelligence operations, allowing Rupprecht to accumulate, unobserved by Allied airplanes or balloons, forty-two divisions and several thousand pieces of heavy artillery—a build-up of attacking forces somewhat like the one that preceded the Battle of the Bulge twenty-six years later.

The man directly responsible for this negligence, however, was General Duchesne, who commanded the defending army in this sector. The general was so oblivious of the German preparations, in fact, that on May 26, the day before the attack broke, he left the front without permission and was seen in Paris in the company of "gay ladies." When news of the assault reached him, he rushed back to his headquarters, but was too late either to halt the onrushing Germans or to save his own reputation. He was relieved of his command shortly afterward and sent to Limoges, the graveyard for disgraced French officers, where it was said they passed the time by telling each other how it had happened. (Similarly disgraced—"benzined"—American officers were sent to Blois—"Bloo-ey" in Yankee-French; although one American general suggested with heavy-handed humor that they be "canned" in Cannes.)

The Germans used a new tactic of massed and speeded attack, which had been developed by General von Hutier on the Russian Front, and achieved complete surprise. Crown Prince Rupprecht, the fifty-year-old descendant of the Stuart kings of Britain, was delighted to see the enemy line practically melt before his eyes. A tactical distraction had become a great strategic victory, and he hastened to exploit it to the utmost. By the morning of May 30—shortly before General Pétain called on Pershing in the latter's headquarters in Chaumont—the nose of the "Bulldog" salient had penetrated more than thirty-five miles from the jump-off line, an impressive gain when you consider that, in so-called "classic" trench warfare, massed armies fought for months to advance a hundred yards.

Pétain's visit marked at least the twentieth time in the past three months that the Allies had come to Pershing for help. Just a few days before, in fact, he had been obliged to lend them the 1st Division. It was now on the Somme, fighting to hold the village of Cantigny, which it had captured on May 28 in the first successful, if very limited, American offensive of the war. This time, too, Pershing had no choice: the situation, he knew, was too critical for halfway measures—even allowing for the French chief of staff's congenital pessimism. So that—although it must have griped his very soul to do it, for of the half-million American troops in France there were only four divisions in anything resembling combat readiness—he agreed to place two of these divisions, the 2nd and 3rd, at Pétain's disposal. But where, he wanted to know, would they be used?

While waiting for Pershing's reply to his request, Pétain had crossed the office to a large map of France hanging on the wall. Now he turned to it and, with his thumbnail, drew a sharp semicircle east of Paris. Here, he said, in the Sixth French Army sector. So great was his tension that his nail actually gouged through the map in two places to the wood paneling beneath. The scale of the map was too small for the name to be indicated, but a fraction of an inch from one of these cuts was a patch of forest, about half the size of New York's Central Park, called Belleau Wood.

CHAPTER 2

ALL day the trucks rolled towards the sound of the guns. They moved in convoys of fifty, each convoy carrying a battalion of the 2nd Division's line regiments, and they raised such thick billowing clouds of dust that, to a friendly aviator circling overhead, they looked like a series of giant white caterpillars undulating along the road.

It was hot and sultry that last day of May, and by mid-morning the sun had turned the interior of each truck into a dust-filled oven. The drivers suffered most from the heat, pinned as they were in closed cabs behind the motors. The troops were luckier. They rolled back the canvas tops, took off their shirts and helmets,

14

and sprawled as comfortably as possible on the hard wooden benches with their rifles and packs and gas masks heaped around their feet.

None of them had more than the vaguest idea of where they were going. Yesterday they had been training in a quiet region of small farms and orchards northwest of Paris, sweating through endless hours of bayonet drill, lectures by visiting experts on the art of the grenade, machine gun, mortar, and other weapons, marching here and there about the countryside in complex divisional maneuvers. Today they were headed towards the front. That was all any of them knew for certain, although all sorts of wild rumors were circulating. But it did not seem to worry them. They were young and healthy, full of animal high spirits, not yet affected by the cynicism and disillusion that had sapped the morale of the French and British and German troops; and they had a touching, childish faith in the omniscience of their officers. Indeed, from the way they behaved they might have been going to a picnic or a ball game rather than to a place where their chances of getting killed or mutilated were better than even. They sang "Tipperary," "Over There," and other popular songs, looked at the green and pleasant countryside gliding past, and yelled cheerful obscenities at pretty girls in the crowds that lined the streets of every town and village through which they passed.

These crowds sprang up as if by magic, waving miniature American flags, throwing flowers, chocolate, bottles of wine into the trucks, cheering *"Vive l'Amérique!"* They too acted as if the Americans were going to a picnic, although the predominance of black garments among them announced clearly that there was hardly a man or woman in France who had not lost at least one relative in the trenches. But the French had good reason to feel pleased. Since their arrival overseas the Americans had done all sorts of work. They had built warehouses, storage plants, barracks, piers; unloaded ships and dredged harbors; repaired railroad tracks and rolling stock; strung telegraph and telephone lines. They had in fact—with the exception of a couple of minor trench raids—done everything but fight. As month after

15

month had passed, the French had begun to feel disillusioned with *"Les Sammies,"* as they called the Americans (a name the Americans abominated, never responded to, and finally succeeded in changing to "Yanks" or "Doughboys"). Now, at last, thirteen months after entering the war, they were going into action. "The spectacle of these magnificent youths from overseas, these beardless children of twenty, radiating strength and health, produced a great effect," a French observer, Jean de Pierrefeu, wrote. "They contrasted strikingly with our regiments in their faded uniforms, wasted by so many years of war, their members thin, their eyes shining with a dull fire, no more than bundles of nerves. . . . We all had the impression that we were about to see a wonderful operation of transfusion of blood. Life was coming in floods to reanimate the dying body of France, almost bled to death." Not all the French exhibited the same degree of enthusiasm, however, for De Pierrefeu overheard one bearded poilu, his uniform still encrusted with the grime of the trenches, mutter cynically, "Go to it, my lads. You won't look like that in a week's time."

Far ahead of the trucks, racing along the road in his staff car, was Colonel Preston Brown, the division chief of staff. The colonel was not nearly as insouciant as the troops. He was in fact badly worried. It was his responsibility to see that the division arrived on schedule with a minimum of confusion and delay, that ammunition, rations, and other supplies were waiting for them, and that the commanding officer on the receiving end, General Duchesne, knew what to do with them when they did arrive. None of this seemed likely to happen as planned. Even in peacetime, as the slim gray-haired colonel knew from experience, it was a formidable task to move twenty-five thousand men from one place to another. Now, at short notice, in an emergency so critical that the French Government was preparing to leave Paris, the difficulties were multiplied many times over. Colonel Brown, in fact, had never seen such a mess.

The colonel's troubles had started at exactly five o'clock the previous evening. He had been in his office in the village of Chaumont-en-Vexin, relaxing over a cup of coffee after a hard day's work, when a dusty French staff car had pulled up outside the farmhouse in which division headquarters was located and a harried-looking major had climbed out and hurried inside.

The major gave Colonel Brown, who spoke French, a brief resume of the situation on the Marne, and told him that the 2nd Division had been placed at the disposal of the Sixth French Army. It was to leave as quickly as possible, he said, for the town of Meaux, about halfway between Paris and Château-Thierry, and take up support positions behind the retreating French. The most pressing need was for line troops, so trucks would arrive within an hour to carry the 3rd Brigade (infantry) and the 4th Brigade (marines) to the front. Transportation would be supplied for the other units— artillery, machine gun, signal, engineers, etc.—if and when it became available, but they were not to count on it. It was more than likely that they would have to move under their own power.

Colonel Brown heard the major out in stunned silence—"with a sick feeling in the pit of my stomach." He took off his green celluloid eyeshade, which gave him the faintly raffish appearance of a dealer in a gambling house, and wiped his forehead. There must be some mistake, he said to the major. The division had received orders early that morning to move north to an assembly point near Beauvais, and from there to relieve the 1st Division on the Somme. He and his staff had spent all day drawing up march tables and issuing the necessary orders. He had even sent advance billeting parties to Beauvais to arrange for quarters.

The major gave a Gallic shrug. That was a shame, he said, but all previous orders had been countermanded by General Foch himself. Colonel Brown would shortly receive written confirmation from A.E.F. headquarters.

Colonel Brown had heard rumors about the German breakthrough to the Marne, but had no concrete information except for the odd bits and pieces he had been able to glean from the circumspect French communiqués—notoriously untrustworthy when they concerned defeats. Just how serious was it, he asked the major.

The major shrugged again. French headquarters, he

said, was in a state of indescribable confusion, struggling to make sense of a welter of conflicting reports. The situation was bad—that was all he could say for certain. Doubtless the colonel would get more up-to-date information in Meaux.

As soon as the major had gone, Colonel Brown called in his aides and buckled down to work. He need not have hurried, however, for French Headquarters was indeed in a state of confusion. Far from arriving "within an hour," as the major had said they would, it was not until four o'clock the following morning that the first trucks, driven by Annamites and Tonkinese from French Indo-China, rattled up the road to the embarkation points. Colonel Brown was grateful for the delay: it gave him and his staff time to accomplish the otherwise impossible task of drawing up new march tables, transmitting the orders to the brigade adjutants, and dealing with the multitude of other details necessary to move the division.

The men in the line regiments (5th and 6th Marines; 9th and 23rd Infantry), however, were less grateful for the delay. From 6:00 P.M. until midnight they were assembled, inspected, marched from one embarkation point to another, and finally, when the trucks failed to appear, bivouacked in the fields alongside the road. They spent a miserable night, protected from the chill, damp air by a single blanket and poncho per man, roused at frequent intervals by false alarms, cursing both the hurry-up-and-wait inefficiency and the premature loss of their warm and comfortable billets.

At six o'clock in the morning, shortly after the first convoys moved off down the road, Colonel Brown drove to Paris and arranged for ammunition, rations, and hospital supplies to be sent ahead. Now, several hours later, yawning repeatedly from fatigue and nervous tension, and oblivious of everything but the logistic problems confronting him, he was on his way to Meaux to prepare for the troops' arrival.

BACK at the training area of which Chaumont-en-Vexin was the nerve center, the rest of the division was getting ready to follow the line regiments to the front.

Several thousand mules, used to haul baggage and ration and ammunition wagons, water carts, and rolling kitchens, as well as cannon and heavy Hotchkiss machine guns, were curried and brushed and given a good feed by their wranglers. The men in the motorized ambulance sections went over their vehicles—six-passenger General Motors ambulances and four-passenger Model-T Fords —seeing to it that they had plenty of gas and oil and water for the journey. Sweating, bare-chested cannoneers limbered up their 75's and 155's, and then unlimbered them again when the harried French transport officer, who was beset by demands of equal urgency from all points of the compass, somehow produced thirty-two trains of the infamous "forty-or-eights" to carry them to the front. The engineers gathered enormous rolls of barbed wire, iron stakes, picks, and long-handled shovels, and loaded them aboard yet another train. Some of them still had in their possession the old wide-brimmed campaign hat, for the new "overseas" cap had just begun to be distributed. They were ordered to turn them in to the quartermaster for salvage: where they were going only steel helmets would be necessary. Emergency rations—two days' supply of corned beef ("canned willie") or bacon, hardtack, sugar, and coffee—were issued and the men warned, upon pain of court-martial, not to eat them unless so ordered. And, lastly, the all-important gas masks were inspected and defective ones replaced.

Major General Omar Bundy, the division commander, remained in Chaumont-en-Vexin until the bulk of these preparations had been completed, then climbed into his car and set off after the line regiments. Bundy was a small dapper man of fifty-odd with an English-style brush mustache, delicate features, and mild, unmilitary eyes. It was he who decided, mistakenly, that cannon would prove more useful than machine guns in the emergency, and assigned the available trains to the artillery regiments. This meant that the machine-gun battalions had to walk, and at seven o'clock that evening they started out on a march that the men were to remember and talk about for years afterward.

Hour after hour they plodded along in the darkness, choked and blinded by the clouds of fine white dust that

19

coated them from head to foot, struggling to control the mules that hauled the guns and ammunition carts. In the distance they could see the flashes of exploding bombs dropped by enemy aircraft, and the resulting fires that flickered red and yellow and orange from the underside of the clouds. On two occasions enemy airplanes passed overhead and the men all looked towards the ground so that the whiteness of their faces would not give the pilots a target (it was a court-martial offense to look upwards in such circumstances). Another time they stopped at a railroad crossing to allow an ambulance train to pass. The moon had risen by then and in its light they could see the blood-stained bandages of the wounded men inside the cars. "We were silent and thoughtful for a good while afterwards," one of their officers noted in his diary.

At eight-thirty the next morning, just beyond l'Isle Adam, they halted for a meal of boiled potatoes, bacon, and coffee. Sanitary men, as the medical corpsmen were called, went down the line caring for sore and blistered feet. After a two-hour break the whistles blew, the men struggled to their feet, adjusted their "Khaki dolls" (packs), and went on until four o'clock in the afternoon, when they made camp for the night by the side of the road. They had covered fifty miles in twenty-one hours, and were still a considerable distance from the front. To their immense relief, trucks arrived the following morning and carried them the rest of the way.

Last to leave Chaumont-en-Vexin was the division's delousing unit. This consisted of two large iron cylinders that were riveted to the chassis of steam-driven trucks. Bundles of clothing and blankets were fed into the cylinders through circular hinged doors at the back. Five pounds of steam pressure and an exposure of fifteen minutes was enough to kill both the lice and their nits. These huge iron-wheeled machines had a maximum speed of four miles an hour and were so heavy that their crews often had to repair roads and reinforce bridges before they could trust them with the weight. The unit was commanded by a sergeant known as "Arkansas Pete," an outsize, Bunyanesque individual who had difficulty finding clothes to fit him, and as a result wore a bizarre assortment of odd bits and pieces of uniform culled from the various Allied armies. He and his men lived a curious nomadic existence, traveling from company to company in the "cootie zone," sleeping in the cylinders (the most sanitary sleeping quarters of any troops at the front), seeing more of the country than anyone else in the division. A number of legends grew up around Arkansas Pete, the most colorful of which concerns his departure from Chaumont-en-Vexin. Apparently, in the rush to move the division to the front, no provision was made to transport the delousing unit by rail. So Pete collected a load of coal, fired up his boilers until they were white hot, gave three loud blasts with his whistle, and started down the road towards Meaux. The great lumbering machines terrified children and livestock, knocked down several shops and houses, and almost destroyed the Royal Tombs in St. Denis; but late that night they pulled up before the quartermaster's billets in a village beyond Meaux and Pete reported for duty, "ready ⟨ ⟩ ⟨ ⟩y delousing emergency."

MEAUX, a provincial capital of some thirteen thousand inhabitants, had been the high-water mark of the German advance in 1914. Now it was inundated once more by a flood of soldiers and civilians that poured into it from all directions. Haggard-eyed, weary refugees drifted aimlessly about the streets accompanied by vehicles of all sizes and descriptions—baby carriages, ox- or horse-drawn wagons, small carts pulled by dogs—which were piled high with bundles of clothing, mattresses, the family treasures of linen and crockery, candlesticks, crucifixes, plaster statues of Our Lady, a prized chair, the inevitable parrot or canary in a cage, and wide-eyed, dirty-faced children. Mounted French couriers charged here and there among them, the shod hoofs of their animals striking sparks from the cobblestones. Sullen Territorials from Algeria and Morocco, their mustard-colored uniforms caked and stained with trench filth, defeat stamped in every line of their faces, trudged through the town. Several hundred German prisoners of war, who had been working on farms in the vicinity, were

21

hastily escorted to the railroad station, shoved aboard a train, and carried away from possible liberation. An endless procession of barges, loaded with refugees, moved prow to stern along the Marne, which flowed through the town. And underscoring the confusion, lending urgency and pattern to the most random movement, was the continual rumble of artillery from the east and the occasional wasplike passage of airplanes overhead.

Into this turmoil streamed the trucks carrying the marines and infantry of the 2nd Division—those, that is, that had not broken down en route, or whose drivers, most of whom had been ferrying troops for seventy-two hours without a break, had not fallen asleep at the wheel and crashed into one of the poplars that lined the Paris-Metz highway. Colonel Brown, watching the trucks arrive, realized that a traffic jam of monumental proportions was in the making, so he went at once to General Duchesne's headquarters a couple of miles to the east (the general had not yet been relieved of his command) and, after some argument, persuaded him to re-route the convoys northeast of the village of Mayen-Multien. This improved matters somewhat, although the road between Meaux and May-en-Multien was clogged with thousands of refugees who reduced the trucks' progress to a crawl. These refugees were astonished to see troops heading in what appeared to be the wrong direction; to these dazed and battered farmers and shopkeepers anyone with sense was moving west. *"La guerre est fini!"* they called to the men in the trucks, gesturing for them to go back the way they had come. Some of the Americans yelled *"Pas fini!"*—a reply which gave a name to the Pasfini sector of the front.

First to arrive at May-en-Multien was a battalion of the 5th Marines under Lieutenant Colonel Frederick Wise. The colonel, a lean, sharp-featured Virginian with black hair and black eyes, was hot, tired, and angry. He had been in Paris, visiting his wife, when the division had received orders to move. Informed of the situation by a telephone call from regimental headquarters, he had borrowed an ambulance from the American Hospital in Neuilly and raced back to his battalion, reaching it just a few minutes before the platoon leaders blew their whistles and the men clambered aboard the trucks. He had missed a night's sleep. He had lost his gear, which was in a truck somewhere behind him. And so far no one had bothered to tell him what was happening.

While his men climbed out of the trucks and moved about to restore circulation to their numb limbs, Wise walked over to a captain of French lancers who was standing nearby, watching the proceedings, and asked him in pidgin French what the situation was at the front. The captain was still struggling to make his reply understood when a messenger from division headquarters came up to Wise with orders for him to march north and occupy the village of Gandelu. Wise formed up his battalion in a column of squads and started out, but he had covered less than two miles when another messenger dashed up on a motorcycle and handed him a note which read: "Return to May at once. Germans have already taken Gandelu."

"God damn it!" Wise snapped to his adjutant, Lieutenant Legendre, "I wish to hell they'd make up their minds!"

The truth was that the French did not know where to send the Americans. The front was in flux, and danger seemed to threaten from a dozen points at once. Was the main German thrust coming from Soissons, Château-Thierry, or somewhere in between? The French High Command could only guess. Their intelligence service, adapted to the relatively stable and slow-moving conditions of the trenches, had broken down, unable to cope with the rapid changes and wide-ranging troop movements of open warfare. Machine-gun units of the 3rd Division were at that moment engaged in a hot fight with the enemy for possession of the bridges over the Marne in Château-Thierry, just a few miles to the southeast. But pressure was being felt from Soissons as well. The French had sent their own reinforcements into the line as quickly as they had arrived—"where," as General Pétain reported to Foch in a splendidly poetic description of horror, "overwhelmed by numbers, they evaporated immediately, like drops of rain on white-hot iron." General Duchesne, faced with chaos and certain disgrace, dithered undecisively. "His headquarters was a

23

scene of panic and despair," one of the 2nd Division's staff officers commented harshly. "While soldiers rushed about here and there, shoving stacks of records into packing crates, and white-faced junior officers babbled over field telephones, the general and his staff held one conference after another."

Duchesne could not make up his mind what to do with the Americans. First he sent them to the VII Corps front facing Soissons, then to the XXI Corps just northwest of Château-Thierry; first he sent them to Mayen-Multien, then to the village of Montreuil-aux-Lions some four miles west of the German salient. By the time these orders were transmitted to the brigade, regiment, and battalion level, entire units of the division were either lost, separated from their officers, or both. Truckloads of rations and ammunition were dumped anywhere; battalions trudged along dusty back roads while their officers frantically sent runners in all directions to try to locate the regimental and brigade commanders. Colonel Albertus W. Catlin, commanding the 6th Marine Regiment, whose experience was typical, wrote of this period: "Then followed a series of misadventures that tried my soul. . . . I was a lost colonel, hunting around in the dark for his command, and hunting with an anxiety that, in this crisis, approached panic."

Nightfall compounded the confusion. The roads were a tangle of trucks, animals, and refugees, none able to move at more than a snail's pace. General Bundy struggled ineffectually to straighten out the mess; then, at midnight, gave up and went to sleep in a nearby farmhouse. Brigadier General James G. Harbord, commanding the marine brigade, worked for several hours longer rounding up units of marines and infantry and getting them turned in the right direction—a task complicated by German aircraft which intermittently bombed the highway. But when he learned that General Bundy ("Little General Bundy," as he invariably referred to him, with unmistakable overtones of contempt) had given it up as a bad job, he passed the word down the line for the troops to bivouac until 4:30 A.M., when they would resume marching to the front; then he turned in for a couple of hours' sleep himself.

Harbord was a tall burly man of fifty-two with sharp blue eyes, a square, jutting jaw, and thin lips, and the wattled "turkey" throat of an outdoorsman. After graduating from Kansas Agricultural College in 1887, he had joined the army as a private and served in every non-commissioned rank before being promoted to second lieutenant. An ambitious, hard-driving man, he was soon marked as a "comer" by his superiors. They pushed him steadily from grade to grade until, in 1917, General Pershing chose him as his chief of staff. Harbord, however, was not happy in this job. For one thing, he considered himself a field officer and was eager for the test of combat; and for another, he found Pershing a difficult man to work for. He was particularly irritated by the commander in chief's lack of time sense. "He is without it as utterly as a color-blind person is without a sense of color," Harbord wrote in his diary, "or a deaf person without music. He is most trying in that respect. An American untried major general may not keep a field marshal waiting or be an hour late to an ambassador's dinner, and those of us around him are forever his guardians and trying to get him over the line on time."

Harbord served as chief of staff until early in May, 1918, when General Doyen, the commanding officer of the marine brigade, was relieved because of illness. There were no other marines of general rank in Europe, so Pershing turned over the command to Harbord, of whom he thought highly. "You are to have charge of the finest body of troops in France," Pershing told him, "and if they fail to live up to that reputation, I shall know whom to blame."

This put Harbord under pressure not only to produce satisfactory results for the commander in chief but also to prove himself to the marines, who had naturally been disappointed when the command was given to an army man rather than to one of their own officers. Even before they went into combat, however, Harbord impressed the marines with his qualities as a commander. "He was first of all a man of action," wrote Colonel Catlin, who had attended the War College with him, "and from the time he took over our force . . . things were always on the move. He was a glutton for work himself and was always inspecting something or somebody. There were no idle units under him. And he exhibited that ideal combination of discipline and democratic attitude which we like to think is typically American. . . . Though not a marine himself, General Harbord fully understood and appreciated the traditions of our corps, and it was said of him that he became as pro-marine as any marine."

And Harbord in turn was favorably impressed by the eight thousand men under his command. He especially admired the easy camaraderie that existed between the officers and the enlisted men. "No marine officer ever pulled any of that 'my man' stuff," he wrote in his diary. "The habitual form of address was 'lad' or 'my lad.' No marine was ever too old to be a 'lad.' . . . Individual marines seemed to have a participating interest in every officer's mess. At our brigade mess there was hot coffee on the fire day and night. All runners received the invitation: 'Go back to the galley, lad, and get a cup of coffee.'" Harbord was impressed, too, by the fact that sixty per cent of the marines were college men, and that almost all the officers from lieutenant on up, and many of the high-ranking noncoms, knew each other by their first names and had served together in the campaigns in Mexico and Central America. Some of them had even served in the Philippines during the Spanish-American War and the insurrection that followed it, and in China during the Boxer Rebellion.

Indeed, at no time in the fighting to come was Harbord ever disappointed in the marines. Rather, it was French defeatism and bungling that infuriated him and that caused him to write in his diary: "It will be a wonder if we do not feel as much like fighting them [the French] as the Germans before the war is over."

EARLY the next morning, June 1, the staff officers of the division reported to the XXI Corps commander, General Degoutte, for instructions. Degoutte, a slim, elegant man who wore pince-nez on a black ribbon and had waxed, sharply pointed mustaches, was almost as badly demoralized as General Duchesne. "The French Commander's opinion was that a retreat should be made," the 2nd Division's regulating officer noted shortly after the conference, "and he evidently considered everything lost and the Germans practically the victors."

Degoutte's first idea was to send the Americans into the line piecemeal, by battalions and companies, as he had the French reinforcements earlier. But General Bundy and Colonel Brown refused. Neither the artillery nor the machine guns had arrived yet, they pointed out. Furthermore, the men had spent up to thirty hours in the trucks, had slept little or none at all for two nights in succession, carried only a hundred and fifty rounds of small arms ammunition apiece, and had already been forced to use their emergency rations, as the rolling kitchens were still far behind. They should be placed on a defensive line supporting the French rear guards. First stop the German advance; then organize a counter-attack. That was the only plan that made sense.

Degoutte mulled over these suggestions for a moment, then tentatively agreed to adopt them. But he was dubious of the Americans' fighting qualities. After all, he said, they were raw, inexperienced troops. How could they be expected to hold against Boche *stürmtruppen,* tough, disciplined soldiers who had consistently gained ground against or, at worst, successfully held off, superior forces throughout the war?

"General Degoutte," Colonel Brown replied indignantly, "these are American regulars. In a hundred and fifty years they have never been beaten. They will hold."

These were brave, eminently quotable words, but they were not the strict truth. The regiments were indeed regular. The 9th had battle honors running back to the Indian Wars of 1856, and had taken part in the march on Peking in 1900. The 23rd, organized in 1861, had fought throughout the Civil War, and had stood at the walls of Manila when the Spaniards surrendered the city in 1898. And the Marine Corps had played a role in every war in America's history. But this was not to say that the men who now composed these regiments were regular. Indeed, with the exception of a few officers and NCO's in the "Syracuse" Brigade (as the 3rd Brigade was known, probably because most of its men had been recruited in upper New York State) and three thousand marine veterans, they were green as grass.

27

General Degoutte, though still dubious, ordered the four regiments to occupy a line straddling the Paris-Metz highway a few miles northwest of Château-Thierry. The 9th was just arriving (frightening the French who, seeing troops in foreign uniform, thought the enemy had encircled them), so it was sent in south of the highway, where the danger seemed most acute. Two battalions of the regiment were spread out thinly over a five-thousand-yard front; the third was held in reserve. German infantry had already occupied a hill just four miles from the village of Coupru, where the XXI Corps headquarters was located, so it was vital that the remaining regiments move up as quickly as possible. Informed of this necessity by a messenger, Harbord raced back along the highway in his staff car, took possession of a number of trucks that were unloading rations and ammunition, filled them with marines, and personally escorted them to the front. Then he reported back to division headquarters, which had been established in the town hall of Montreuil-aux-Lions.

While he was there, talking over the situation with General Bundy and Colonel Brown, a French officer raced up on a motorcycle from corps headquarters. "General Degoutte sends his compliments," he said. "He asks that the division commander put in another regiment without delay."

General Bundy, his cavalryman's boots and Sam Browne belt gleaming and his uniform as neatly pressed as though he were going on parade, turned to Colonel Brown. "Send in the Twenty-third Infantry."

But Colonel Brown was unable to locate the 23rd; it was somewhere on the road between May-en-Multien and the VII Corps sector, to which General Duchesne had originally assigned it. So Bundy said to Harbord: "General Harbord, you will have to put in one of your regiments."

"I am very glad to put in one of my regiments, General," Harbord replied. "But I hope you will not split my brigade in its first action. Can't you let the Paris-Metz highway be the dividing line between the two brigades and let me place my regiment north of the road—its right connecting with the left of the Ninth Infantry?"

General Bundy agreed, and so it was more by accident than by design or foresight that the marines found themselves directly opposite the nose of the "Bulldog" salient, the most advanced point of the German drive towards Paris. This virtually guaranteed them heavy fighting in the immediate future, for, as innumerable veterans of the war have pointed out in diaries, letters, memoirs, and formal histories, it was common practice to "bite off a salient because of a passion for straight lines in G.H.Q."

CHAPTER 3

WHILE the marines and infantry trudged through the sun-drenched fields near Château-Thierry, their shoulders instinctively hunched and their heads bowed against the roar of artillery and the chatter of machine guns that now came with disconcerting clearness across No Man's Land, the Supreme War Council was preparing to hold its sixth session in Versailles. A parade of gleaming black limousines, each preceded by its motorcycle escort, streamed down the tree-lined highway from Paris and pulled up in front of the Grand Trianon Château, where they disgorged prime ministers, field marshals, admirals, and a profusion of high government officials. Clemenceau, the aging "Tiger of France," seemed calm and unruffled as he trotted across the pavement swinging his cane; Lloyd George, his leonine mane stirred by the breeze, spoke earnestly with Viscount Milner and Foreign Minister Arthur Balfour; Orlando, the Italian premier, was seen to scowl angrily as he discussed something with Baron Sidney Sonnino, his foreign minister.

Junior members of the delegations clustered in excited groups in front of the château, speculating among themselves about the situation at the front and anxiously seeking the latest news from arriving officers. It was generally feared that this would be the last session of the Council in Versailles. The next one—if there was a next one—might be held in Tours or Bordeaux, even, it was whispered, in London. But their spirits were given a lift by Colonel William Wallace, one of General Bliss's staff, when he told them he had just returned from Meaux and had seen units of the 2nd Division hastening towards the front.

General Bliss himself, a portly man of sixty-five with a bushy white mustache, pince-nez, and usually with a swagger stick tucked under one arm, was rather pessimistic about the Allies' prospects. He had ordered all his official papers crated and had several trucks standing by to transport them to safety at a moment's notice. And he wrote to his wife: "It seems strange to walk in the quiet and peace of my garden, watch the stars twinkling through the elms and the birch trees, and at the same time hear the dull booming of the cannonade to the eastwards, showing how near the war is to Paris. But you must not worry. Our plans are all made in case we should have to leave. . . . A few more days will probably decide."

Bliss had served as chief of staff to General James Wilson during the Puerto Rican campaign in 1898, and as governor of Moro Province in the Philippines, and had helped draw up the mobilization plans after the United States had declared war. In 1917 he was appointed Army chief of staff, but was soon replaced by General Peyton March, a harder and more efficient individual, and kicked upstairs to his present post. For a high-ranking professional military man, Bliss was remarkably indecisive. One of the main reasons he had been relieved of his job as chief of staff was his unfortunate habit of hiding important papers beneath his desk blotter until he decided what to do about them. This indecisiveness was no handicap in the Supreme War Council, however, for the daily decisions that spelled the difference between victory and defeat were not usually made in the "word factory" in Versailles, but in the individual Allied headquarters. After the war Bliss served as unofficial American representative to the League of Nations and became known as "The Peacemaker" for his efforts to have Germany and Russia included in that ill-fated precursor of the United Nations.

The atmosphere in the conference room itself was tense and solemn—"of those in a house of prayer and grievous illness, when the members, suppressing their alarm, automatically go about their routine as a relief from their suspense." Although everyone's thoughts were on the battle shaping up a few miles to the east, the battle that would decide the fate of Paris and possibly of the war, the Council resolutely followed an agenda that had been previously decided upon.

One of the first items brought under discussion was a proposal to unify the Adriatic Fleet under one command in order to meet the threat now posed by the combined Austrian, Turkish, and Russian navies. Orlando rejected this in short order. Italy, he said vehemently, had only five battleships and she proposed to keep them safe in harbor so long as one Austrian battleship was afloat and there was no better evidence than that now being shown on the Marne that the Allies would be victorious. There was obviously no possibility that he would change his mind, so the subject was shelved for the indefinite future. Then the British renewed their proposal to send an expedition to Siberia to help the White Russians, Admiral Kolchak and General Denikin, who were still fighting there against the Bolsheviks. While this was being thrashed out, amid mutual recriminations, General Bliss stepped out into the corridor for a breath of air. He was joined by tall, gangling Sir Henry Wilson, the British chief of staff, who asked him, "How are they getting on in there?"

"Still all at sea except for the Italian Navy," Bliss replied, then hurriedly cautioned Wilson, who was guffawing loudly, not to repeat the remark lest it reach the ears of the Italians and cause bad feelings. Since Caporetto, the Italians had become very sensitive to criticism.

Later in the morning, after Bliss had returned to the conference room and taken his seat beside General Pershing, Clemenceau introduced what he felt to be the main business of the Council: the assigning of future American reinforcements. Pershing, however, knew that

31

this was merely another stratagem in the Allies' campaign to prevent the formation of an independent American Army, so he insisted that the disposition of United States troops was not within the province of the Council to determine. Instead, he suggested a private meeting in Clemenceau's office with Clemenceau, Lloyd George, Milner, and Generals Foch and Weygand. Clemenceau and Lloyd George were scheduled for a closed session with Orlando that morning, so the conference began with only Pershing, Milner, and the two French generals present.

No sooner had the door to Clemenceau's office been closed and a guard posted outside, than Foch launched into a tirade, the substance of which was that only infantry and machine gunners—250,000 men per month—should be sent from America during June and July. The future Marshal of France, a stocky, ebullient man with a walrus mustache and the eyes of a shrewd peasant, was in a shaky position. He was being sharply criticized for not having anticipated the German thrust in the Chemin des Dames and for having sent reinforcements north to Amiens in the stubborn conviction that the heavy fighting would continue to take place there. Some of the Deputies were asking embarrassing questions in the Chamber, and others had even dared to suggest that Foch was losing his grip and should be replaced. The general badly needed a victory, even a minor one, to placate the politicians.

Pershing, however, was unwilling to play the sacrificial lamb; he had his own plans and ambitions to further. General Foch's policy, he replied, was shortsighted and dangerous. He fully realized the gravity of the situation, but the American organization must nevertheless be built up and rounded out in order to carry on the battle to the end. Foch's proposal would leave the Americans two hundred thousand men short of enough to complete combat units and fill up special organizations of the S.O.S. (Service of Supply). He went on to speak of the deplorable condition of the French railroads and port facilities, and of the need for skilled workmen to repair and maintain them.

32

As Pershing continued to expound in his slow, professorial manner, as though he were addressing a rather stupid child, Foch grew visibly more and more agitated, turned red in the face, and finally burst out, waving his arms in the air: "The battle! The battle! Nothing else counts!"

At this point Lloyd George and Clemenceau came in, and Lloyd George, who had caught only Foch's last words, immediately spoke up. "I think President Wilson will be deeply interested in General Foch's views," he said. As America had no Prime Minister present, he added (with the clear implication that Pershing, a mere general, was meddling in things in which he had no right to meddle, and was, in fact, impudently contradicting his superiors), he thought it would be "inconvenient" to make a decision and that the question should be brought before the entire Council.

Pershing bluntly refused to consider this. (He knew very well that once he accepted the Council's hegemony over American troops, he might as well resign his command.) Furthermore, he said, President Wilson had been embarrassed by the representations made to him personally by the French and British ambassadors and by Monsieur Viviani, Clemenceau's special envoy to Washington. The President was trusting to his, Pershing's, judgment in the matter.

At an impasse, the meeting was adjourned until the following afternoon, June 2, when once again Lloyd George, Clemenceau, and Foch employed every argument at their command to force Pershing's capitulation. "Are you willing to take the risk?" Foch asked him repeatedly, and Pershing replied that he was ready to assume any responsibility that his proposal might entail (including, presumably, the loss of Paris to the enemy), but that he must have a greater proportion of auxiliary troops to keep America's organization from "going to smash."

Faced with this invincible *sang-froid,* Foch threw his hands in the air and fell silent. Then Pershing turned to Clemenceau and asked him what he thought the results would be if Paris fell. Clemenceau replied that he and Lloyd George had discussed that possibility and had decided that they would go on fighting, for "above Paris is France, and above France is all the civilized world to save."

This was not Pershing's opinion, nor the opinion of most of the French High Command. They did not discuss the matter openly, of course ("defeatist" officers were swiftly relieved of their commands), but they had dropped enough hints in intimate conversations to leave no doubt of their belief that the loss of Paris would cause an upheaval in the government, drive Clemenceau out of office, and France out of the war.

As Pershing turned to leave, he said to Clemenceau: "Well, Mr. President, it may not look encouraging just now, but we are certain to win in the end."

The Premier clutched him by the hand, and in a tone which belied his assurance of the moment before, said, "Do you really think that? I am glad to hear you say it."

Pershing was touched. "That was the first and only time that I ever sensed any misgivings in Clemenceau's mind," he wrote in his memoirs.

In a final effort to circumvent the American Commander-in-Chief, Clemenceau, Lloyd George, and Orlando composed a joint telegram to President Wilson, which read:

We desire to express our warmest thanks to President Wilson for the remarkable promptness with which American aid, in excess of what at one time seemed possible, has been rendered to the Allies during the past month to meet a great emergency. The crisis, however, still continues. General Foch has presented to us a statement of the utmost gravity, which points out that the numerical superiority of the enemy in France, where 162 Allied divisions now oppose 200 German divisions, is very heavy; and that as there is no possibility of the British and French increasing the number of their divisions—on the contrary, they are put to extreme straits to keep them up—there is a great danger of the war being lost unless the numerical inferiority of the Allies can be remedied as rapidly as possible by the advent of American troops. He therefore urges with the utmost insistence that the

34

maximum possible number of infantry and machine gunners, in which respect the shortage of men on the side of the Allies is most marked, should continue to be shipped from America in the months of June and July to avert the immediate danger of an Allied defeat in the present campaign owing to the Allied reserves being exhausted before those of the enemy. In addition to this, and looking to the future, he represents that it is impossible to see ultimate victory in the war unless America is able to provide such an army as will enable the Allies ultimately to establish numerical superiority. He places the total American force required for this at no less than a hundred divisions.

A hundred divisions, with their complement of auxiliary troops, was over four million men—more than France had put into the field at any one time during the entire war. It would appear that General Foch's respect for the fighting prowess of the Germans, initially high enough, had increased geometrically over the years! Nevertheless, in response to this telegram the War Department planned to send three million troops to France by March, 1919.

"NO retirement will be thought of on any pretext whatsoever," read the order that General Degoutte issued to all the divisions, both French and American, under his command on the afternoon of June 2. But the French, outnumbered and demoralized, most of them not yet recovered from the beating they had taken in the north, continued to give ground steadily. They filtered back across the fields, now waist-high in bright green winter wheat and starred with thousands of scarlet poppies, through the woods and over the streams, past the deserted farms and villages (which they paused to loot) with their untended livestock and abandoned dogs and cats. Some of them retreated in orderly fashion, fighting as they went; others fled in panic, leaving a trail of discarded rifles, packs, clothing, ammunition, even rations for the advancing Germans to gather and distribute among themselves.

The 2nd Division meanwhile, thanks to General Duchesne's vacillation, was still sorting itself out in a kind of gigantic game of musical chairs. Battalions of marines and infantry trudged this way and that, looking for their positions on poorly marked maps. "Where's this here line we're supposed to hold, Sarge?" one tired marine recruit was heard to ask. The sergeant, a grizzled veteran of twenty years' service, grinned at him. "We're gonna make a line, sonny." Only the 9th Infantry and part of the 5th Marines were in position. The 23rd was still in the VII Corps sector several miles north of the position it was eventually to hold, and the 6th Marines was moving up from Montreuil-aux-Lions towards the village of Lucy-le-Bocage, directly opposite the nose of the salient.

Colonel Wise's battalion of the 5th had spent the previous night bivouacked near a farmhouse about halfway between Montreuil-aux-Lions and the front. Shortly before noon Colonel Wendell Neville, the regimental commander (later commandant of the Marine Corps), drove up in his staff car and told Wise to establish a defensive line from the northeast corner of Veuilly Wood to a point east and south of Les Mares Farm. "The French are holding from the railroad on your front," he said to Wise, "but we don't expect them to stick. If you don't hurry, the Germans will get there before you do. And when you get there, you stick! Never mind how many French come through you."

"Who'll be supporting my flanks?" Wise asked him.

"I'll let you know as soon as I know myself," Neville replied, then put the car in gear and shot off down the road.

Less than an hour later Wise's battalion marched up a narrow dirt road, deployed along the designated line, and began to dig in. On their right front was a wide expanse of wheat fields that rose in a gentle slope to a wooded hill (Hill 165) about half a mile distant. Woods and fields swung away behind them on both flanks. And on their left front, tucked in a fold of ground, they could see the red-roofed house and barn of Les Mares Farm. A company of blue-uniformed Chasseurs was camped beside it. There were other French units be-

36

tween them and the enemy, but they had no idea how many.

The men dug in with bayonets, mess kits, and spoons, because the engineers had not yet arrived with entrenching tools, and they wasted no time, for German light artillery—77-millimeter "whiz-bangs," which gave about two seconds warning of their approach, and 88-millimeter "quick Dicks," which gave no warning at all—were already probing the area and causing a few casualties. "It's amazing how quickly we dug in, considering we had no shovels," one marine private wrote. "All around me I saw my buddies sinking slowly into the ground, while parapets of soft earth grew steadily up beside them. . . . We were duly grateful that the Heinies hadn't started dropping their nine-inch 'sea bags' on us. . . ."

The troops' biggest problem, however, was hunger. They had nearly exhausted their iron rations, and the rolling kitchens were still far behind. Early in the afternoon a supply of French rations was brought up to them, but these proved practically inedible. The main item was cans of Argentine corned beef, called "monkey meat" by the French. The beef had spoiled before being canned and it smelled like "a combination of coal oil and putrid mule." It had to be thoroughly heated, preferably with the addition of vegetables, salt, and pepper, to make it at all palatable; but the men were forbidden to build fires so close to the enemy lines, and, hungry as they were, they could not gag it down cold. They ransacked the nearby village of Marigny, where Colonel Wise had established his post of command, but found only a plentiful supply of wine and cider and a few jars of home-preserved fruits, so most of them sprawled in their "graves"—rifle pits 6 feet long, 2½ feet wide, and 3 feet deep—and rolled innumerable cigarettes from sacks of Bull Durham to still their hunger pangs.

The men of another battalion of the 5th were luckier. They came across an abandoned heifer grazing in a field some distance behind the lines, where cooking fires were allowed. Forbidden by an officer to butcher the "Allied" animal, they tethered it in a clump of woods that was under enemy bombardment, and a short while later

37

they were happily carving steaks from the "casualty."

At about 4:00 P.M. Colonel Wise and Lieutenant Legendre made a tour of the battalion's positions. Wise was badly worried. Colonel Neville had telephoned an hour before to say that the 6th Marines would support his right flank and the 23rd Infantry his left. So far neither of them had showed up. To make matters worse, the battalion was stretched out over a two-mile front— far too thin to be effective; it had almost no supporting artillery, for only a couple of the division's batteries had arrived and most of the French batteries had pulled back; and the Germans seemed to be increasing the intensity of their bombardment. Were they preparing to attack?

About half a mile to the south, in the second story of a farmhouse in the village of La Voie du Chatel, Colonel Catlin and his adjutant, Major Frank Evans, audibly wondered the same thing. They had an unobstructed view of Wise's position, and through their field glasses they could see clouds of dust and smoke rising where the enemy shells exploded. Catlin sent a runner back to the lead battalion of the 6th with orders for them to move up on the double and dig in on Wise's exposed right flank. (The 23rd Infantry, which was supposed to protect his left flank, was still in the VII Corps sector, several miles to the northwest, so this role was filled by a battalion of French troops. By the time they arrived, however, the engagement was over.)

More and more shells began dropping into Wise's position. Most of them, fortunately, landed in the woods behind the line of rifle pits. Two French batteries of 75's, the only ones remaining near Wise's post of command, fired a last salvo and then limbered up and departed for safer positions farther back. "They didn't stop to say good-bye," Wise wryly remarked later. The marines hunched down grimly in their pits, shoved a round into the chambers of their Springfield '03's and Chauchat automatic rifles ("Sho-sho" or "Sure-shot" when they worked; less complimentary terms when, as often happened, they jammed), and waited. Even the greenest rookie among them realized they were on the receiving end of a preliminary barrage.

A few minutes later a battalion of Senegalese, huge blue-black men in mustard-colored uniforms, came running back across the fields beyond their left flank. Most of them had thrown away their weapons. Wise, crouched in a ditch beside his post of command, gave a snort of disgust at the sight. "Maybe the English Channel will stop them," he said to Lieutenant Legendre. Then the Chasseurs from Les Mares Farm came marching past. Their commanding officer went up to Captain Lloyd Williams, one of Wise's company commanders, and said that he had written orders for everybody to retreat.

"Retreat, hell!" Williams replied. "We just got here!"

When the last French units had come through the marines' lines and there was nothing between them and the enemy but empty woods and fields, an eerie silence fell over the scene. It lasted for perhaps thirty seconds, and was so profound that the marines could hear blackbirds cawing in a nearby field. Then, from the woods on their right front, German machine guns opened up and, moments later, two columns of German infantry moved out into the wheat fields.

The Germans came slowly and steadily, keeping a good distance between each column, with the sun glinting from their helmets and bayonets. It was the first time any of the marines had seen the enemy, and not a man fired as they watched them approach. Wise tried to spot their leaders but was unable to do so, for the experienced German officers and noncoms had removed their badges of rank. "If this damned line extends beyond our flanks," he said to Legendre, "we're in trouble."

Colonel Catlin and Major Evans had a "box seat" for the show, and both of them later described it. "They came out, on a wonderfully clear day, in two columns across a wheat field," wrote Major Evans in a letter to Major General Barnett, commandant of the Marine Corps. "From our distance it looked flat and green as a baseball field, set between a row of woods on the farther side, and woods and a ravine on the near side. We could see the two thin, brown columns advancing in perfect order until two-thirds of the columns, we judged, were in view. The rifle and machine-gun fire were incessant and overhead the shrapnel was bursting. Then the shrapnel came on the target at each shot. It broke just over and just ahead of those columns and then the next burst sprayed over the very green in which we could see the columns moving. It seemed for all the world that the green fields had burst out in patches of white daisies. . . . And it did it again and again, no barrage but with the skill and accuracy of a cat playing with two brown mice that she could reach and mutilate at will and without any hurry. The white patches would roll away and we could see that some of the columns were still there, slowed up, and it seemed perfect suicide for them to try.

"You couldn't begrudge a tribute to their pluck at that. Then, under that deadly fire and the barrage of rifle and machine-gun fire, the Boche stopped. It was too much for any men. They buried in or broke to the cover of the woods and you could follow them by the ripples of the green wheat as they raced for cover. The 5th bore the brunt of it and on our left the men raked the woods and ravines to stop the Boche at his favorite trick of infiltrating through. An aeroplane was overhead checking up on our artillery's fire and when the shrapnel lay down on those columns . . . the French aviator signalled back to our lines 'Bravo!' The French, who were in support of the 5th, . . . could not, and can not today, grasp the rifle fire of the men. That men should fire deliberately and use their sights, and adjust their range, was beyond their experience. The rifle fire certainly figured heavily in the toll we took, and it must have had a telling effect on the morale of the Boche, for it was something they had not counted on. As a matter of fact, after pushing back the weakened French and then running up against a stone wall defense, they were literally up in the air and more than stopped. We found that out later from prisoners, for the Germans never knew that we were in the front line when they made that attack. They were absolutely mystified at the manner in which the defense had stiffened up until they found out that our troops were in line. . . ."

Colonel Catlin's description, written for public consumption, was even more purple and highly charged than his adjutant's. "If the German advance had looked beautiful to me," he wrote, "that metal curtain that our marines rang down on the scene was even more so. The German lines did not break; they were broken. The Boche fell by the scores there among the wheat and the poppies. They hesitated, they halted, they withdrew a space. Then they came on again. They were brave men; we must grant them that. Three times they tried to re-form and break through that barrage, but they had to stop at last. The United States Marines had stopped them. Thus repulsed with heavy losses they retired, but our fire was relentless; it followed them to their death. . . ."

Colonel Catlin's hyperbole was justified in one respect: although the battle was small in scale (less than a thousand men were engaged on both sides) and short in duration, the marines *had* stopped the Germans at their closest point to Paris since the United States had entered the war. It remained to be seen, however, if they would fare as well against the five divisions that the Germans were massing on their front.

CHAPTER 4

DURING the next two days and nights, while the French continued to retreat, the 2nd Division completed its movement to the front and, after much confusion and shifting about, finally occupied a sector eight thousand yards long and curved to fit the southwest bulge of the enemy salient. Colonel Neville's 5th Marines held the left of the line; next to them on the right, directly opposite the nose of the salient, was the 6th Marines under Colonel Catlin; then, south of the Paris-Metz highway, were the 23rd and 9th Infantry, in that order.

The division's artillery brigade—two regiments of 75's and one of 155's—was in support, as were three battalions of French artillery. One machine-gun battalion was attached to each line regiment, and the engineers were divided between the marines and the infantry, a battalion to each brigade, for entrenching duty. They supplied barbed wire and stakes, wire cutters, picks and shovels, and, when necessary, their rifles and bayonets. The marines, filled to the brim with *esprit de corps,* were generally contemptuous of the army troops, a phenomenon which was also remarked in World War II and the Korean War; but this contempt did not apply to the engineers, who worked and fought side by side with them on many occasions in the days ahead. As one marine corporal remarked: "They dig trenches and mend roads all night, and they fight all day. And when us guys get all killed off, they come up and take over the war. There's no better folks anywhere than the engineers!"

Code names were assigned to all units: CUSTER to the division itself; BOSTON to the infantry brigade; MOSCOU to the marines. The signal battalion worked day and night stringing miles of telephone wire between the various headquarters and advanced outposts—a dangerous and endless task, for the wire was constantly being cut by artillery—and both French and American operators took their places at the switchboards. The Military Police guarded ration and ammunition dumps and directed traffic at the crossroads—also very dangerous work, for the crossroads were favorite targets of the enemy artillery. (One of these M.P.'s, asked by a marine what his job was, replied, "To keep you gyrenes from running away," and was promptly knocked out by a rifle butt. The marine was court-martialed and confined to quarters—a meaningless punishment in the circumstances.)

Esquadrille Squadron 252 of the French Air Force was attached to the division, and three times a day—at dawn, between 9:00 and 10:00 A.M., and just before sunset—a pilot-observer took off from a nearby field and flew low along the front to determine the position of both the American and the German lines. When he fired a rocket of six stars, which meant "Where are you?", the Americans were instructed to mark their positions with a display of panels, handkerchiefs, and other readily distinguishable objects. This worked better in theory than in practice, however, for the troops were usually too busy to comply with the instructions. Indeed, as German aircraft also appeared overhead at frequent intervals, they sometimes fired at the French plane by mistake—even though it was marked by a pennant flying from the left wing. Other rocket signals, from ground to air, were arranged to cover such contingencies as "friendly artillery is firing on us," "gas," "request for barrage," etc.

Despite the success of Colonel Wise's battalion on the afternoon of June 2, the French commanders were still very uncertain of the caliber of the American troops. When a French officer, for example, saw a working party of engineers withdrawing from the 6th Marines' sector on the morning of June 3, he immediately reported that "the right is giving way." This report was relayed in rapid succession to Degoutte's headquarters, then to General Bundy, General Harbord, and finally to Colonel Catlin. Catlin investigated, learned how the rumor had started, and replied caustically: "When my outfit runs it will be in the other direction. Nothing doing in the fall back business."

French distrust, however, keyed the American commanders to a high pitch of tension and they cracked down hard on their officers and NCO's, weeding out those unfit for combat duty. In the 9th Infantry, for example, a major commanding a battalion was relieved because of inability to read a map, and a captain for general inefficiency. Men thus relieved were known as "T.B.'s"— "Throw Backs"—and were usually sent to the Service of Supply. The more hopeless cases were shipped back to the States.

Although six days went by before the rolling kitchens produced their first hot meal, the ration situation was eased somewhat by the arrival of ample stores of "monkey meat," round loaves of coarse hard bread, and cans of beans and tomatoes. Solidified alcohol—"Sterno" —was in short supply, but the men learned to build smokeless fires by breaking up candles in a tin can and using a length of twine for a wick. One of their favorite dishes was "trench doughnuts," which they made by frying bread in bacon grease and sprinkling it liberally with sugar. But water had become a problem. The nearest supply was over a mile away, and runners carrying as many as twenty canteens each made the round trip two or three times a day. Colonel Catlin found something "irresistibly ludicrous" in the sight of these clanking young men hurrying back and forth, while the rest of the troops continued their feverish preparations for combat.

While this work was going on in the American lines, the Germans had driven forward against light French opposition and occupied Belleau Wood and the nearby villages of Torcy, Belleau, Bussiares, and Bouresches. Their heavy artillery, which had been left behind by the unexpectedly rapid advance of the infantry, had caught up, and now the deep-throated roar of 150's (called "Jack Johnsons" because of the quantities of black smoke that hovered in the air when the shell exploded) and the huge 210-millimeter *minenwerfer* (trench mortar), which blasted a crater five feet deep and fifteen feet in diameter, was added to the shriller voices of the 77's and 88's. The Germans increased the tempo of their bombardment, using both high-explosive and gas shells, concentrating their fire on crossroads, rear echelon troop and supply areas, and farmhouses that seemed likely to contain headquarters personnel. Both General Harbord and Colonel Catlin had narrow escapes when their first posts of command were shelled, and Catlin's next headquarters, near the village of Lucy-le-Bocage, was so heavily bombarded that "you could scoop up handfuls of shrapnel bullets in the streets—round pellets about the size of marbles." The shelling caused some two hundred casualties on June 3-4, and a German patrol picked up the body of a dead marine and carried it back to their headquarters, thus obtaining positive identification of their opponents. Until then they had had no idea that American troops were in the line.

The following day, in another barrage, a marine sergeant brought in two wounded Germans under fire. They identified themselves as members of the 7th Saxon Jaeger Regiment of the 197th Division. Both of them were wearing French artilleryman's breeches, which they said had been issued to them by their own quartermaster. (This blossomed in American headlines as HUNS WEARING FRENCH UNIFORMS TO DECEIVE YANKS.)

44

But the enemy did not press home the attack. The active front had moved north to the Noyon-Montdidier sector, and the German IV Reserve Corps (called "Corps Conta" after its commanding officer, General von Conta) had been ordered to protect the left flank of the Seventh German Army in its drive southwest from Soissons. To accomplish this, the corps was to advance to "a position that is especially suited for defense." The advance would be made by five divisions. (It should be noted here that German, French, and British divisions were half the size of American divisions, and that at this stage of the war, when their manpower reserves were all but depleted, many of the German divisions were no larger than an American regiment.) Reconnaissance and preparations were to start at once, but the attack would not be made before June 7. "Corps Conta," read an order to the troops issued on June 4, ". . . is compelled temporarily to assume the defensive, after positions most suitable for this purpose are captured. . . . The offensive spirit must be maintained, even though a temporary lull in the attack seems to exist. In the general picture of the operations, no halt or lull exists. We are the victors and will remain on the offensive. The enemy is defeated."

The overemphatic tone of this order is an obvious clue to the German General Staff's nervous and uncertain state of mind. Despite their impressive gains since the spring, and their momentary numerical superiority, they were far from being the victors. They had suffered enormous losses in their two assaults against the British to the north—losses that were only partially replaced by fresh drafts from Germany; the civilian populace, appalled by the long lists of "killed in action," by the number of armless and legless young men they saw in the streets, by the shortage of everything from butter to bandages (paper bandages were now in general use), and fed up with the other hardships in a nation that was slowly and surely being strangled by the British blockade, was becoming increasingly vociferous in its complaints; and the *Friedenstürm* (Peace Offensive), which the German diplomats had launched in an effort to wrest a favorable treaty from the Allies, was getting nowhere.

Add to this the constantly increasing flow of American troops and matériel into France, and they had little enough cause for optimism.

GENERAL HARBORD had established his first post of command at Issonge Farm, about two miles from the front on a secondary road that joined the Paris-Metz highway. Retreating French troops had looted it and the floor was inches deep in discarded clothing, broken crockery, and the contents of every cupboard and chest of drawers in the place. The owner, a prosperous farmer and stock raiser who had fled with his family several days before, returned a short while after Harbord had moved in. He was not surprised, he told the general, at the condition of his home. He had been there when the troops had burst in and begun looting. He had foolishly remonstrated with them and they had tied him over a chair and beaten him severely.

Harbord did not stay long at Issonge Farm. Two days after he had established his headquarters there, a large-caliber shell landed in the courtyard, killing several horses and wounding two men. That same day he packed up and moved south to a more isolated farmhouse called La Loge. He shared it with Colonel Manus McCloskey, commander of the 12th Field Artillery Regiment. McCloskey, Harbord commented, must have recruited his headquarters staff from Yale, for it included four former members of the Yale Banjo Club. "To the ensemble talent," he wrote, "I contributed my aide, Fielding S. Robinson, who played the guitar and had brought one to war with him. Pell Foster, an officer of one of the batteries, joined with the violin. Nearly every evening we had music." In a sort of ominous postscript to the above, Harbord added: "But the 12th Field Artillery made other music."

At three o'clock on the afternoon of June 5, just a couple of hours after he had moved into La Loge, Harbord received a telephone call telling him to report at once to division headquarters for orders. "We've got work for your marines," Colonel Brown said.

The colonel, looking tired but excited, met Harbord at the door to the *mairie* and led him inside. General

Degoutte, he said, had placed fresh troops on the division's flanks—the French 167th Division on the left and the 10th Colonial on the right—and had issued orders to counterattack before the enemy could consolidate his gains and resume the advance. Accordingly, at three-forty-five the following morning the 167th was to seize the high ground northwest of Belleau Wood. It would be accompanied in this attack by a battalion of the 5th Marines under Major Julius Turrill. (It is further evidence of the French lack of confidence in the Americans that the corps commander should so concern himself with the deployment of a single battalion under his command.) Later in the day, Colonel Brown continued, when these objectives had been attained, the rest of the marine brigade would attack the nose of the salient just beyond Lucy-le-Bocage, capture Belleau Wood, and occupy the high ground overlooking the villages of Belleau and Torcy.

Harbord spent some time with Colonel Brown, going over details, then drove to corps headquarters in Chamigny, seven miles back, to get detailed maps of the objectives, in particular Belleau Wood. To his astonishment and indignation, he learned that no such maps existed. The French offered a curious excuse for this oversight: the Topographical Section and the *Deuxième Bureau* (Intelligence), they said, could not agree whose responsibility it was to make them. The available maps were small in scale and showed only that Belleau Wood was a kidney-shaped patch of forest, slightly elevated above the surrounding fields, which began half a mile south of the eleventh-century village of Belleau (so named for the "beautiful water" that flowed from a nearby spring).

The wood was about a mile and a half long and half a mile wide, with the southern lobe of the "kidney" swinging west towards Lucy-le-Bocage. A long shallow ravine, called Gobert, entered the southern lobe of the wood and would facilitate the attack in this sector. (It became known as "Gob Gully" to the marines.) The approach to the central and northern sections, however, was across wide expanses of wheat fields. "But you should not have any trouble capturing it," Degoutte's intelligence officer reassured Harbord. "It is lightly held by a very short line across the northeast corner."

Harbord had no confidence in this casual appraisal of the situation, but was obliged to accept it for lack of another. Nevertheless, when he returned to his headquarters late that evening, he telephoned Colonel Neville and Colonel Catlin and asked them what reconnaissance they had made of the enemy positions. The 5th had made none at all, Neville replied. It was no excuse, he realized, but he had assumed that the French, who had been occupying Belleau Wood only a few days before, knew all there was to be known about it and had passed on their information to Division Intelligence.

Catlin's news was no better. He said that his intelligence officer, Lieutenant William Eddy, had led a two-man patrol through the enemy's lines the night before. The patrol had lain for hours in a clover field near Torcy, listening to German troops talk as they filed past on the road. It was a dare-devil stunt and he had recommended Eddy for a medal, but the patrol had brought back little in the way of valuable information.

Harbord was disappointed, but did not reprimand his regimental commanders: he had operated on the same assumption as Neville. He chalked it up to "inexperience." But faced with this lack of concrete information and detailed maps, his plan of attack was necessarily simple and straightforward, allowing for a maximum of improvisation on the part of the regimental and battalion commanders. The plan he finally decided upon was this: at 5:00 P.M. the next day a battalion of the 5th Marines under Major Benjamin Berry would move straight east against the northern mass of Belleau Wood; on Berry's right a battalion of the 6th under Major Berton Sibley would take the southern lobe of the wood, then move on, if possible, and capture Bouresches. On Sibley's right another battalion of the 6th, under Major Thomas Holcomb (commandant of the Marine Corps from 1936 to 1943), would keep pace with Sibley's advance and maintain contact with the left of the infantry brigade. Colonel Catlin would direct the attack. Since the wood was believed "lightly held" by the enemy, there would be only a brief artillery barrage before the troops went over the top.

Harbord had at least one thing to be grateful for: his marines were in splendid condition, both physically and psychologically. They thought of themselves as America's élite troops, and were eager for a crack at "Kaiser Bill and his Huns." Along with almost everyone else in the United States, they believed the horror stories told about the Germans in "Bleeding Belgium"—cutting off children's hands, raping nuns, etc.—and they believed, too, that as part of the official German policy of *schrechlichkeit* (frightfulness) that had led them to introduce flame throwers and poison gas into the "art of war," the enemy troops deliberately and cruelly employed a saw-toothed bayonet. There was, in fact, one saw-toothed bayonet in each German squad, but it was used only for sawing wood. No German soldier would dare carry it into battle: it would mean a horrible death if he were taken prisoner with it in his possession. The French bayonet, a sixteen-inch sliver of steel affectionately called "Rosalie" by the poilus, was a far crueler weapon, for it left a puncture that closed up and usually festered.

ABOUT the time that General Harbord was talking with his regimental commanders on the telephone, a forty-six-year-old German major named Bischoff, commanding a regiment of the 237th Infantry Division, was making an informal inspection of his positions in Belleau Wood. Major Bischoff, a veteran of the bush fighting in Africa and a masterful tactician, had performed prodigies of labor in the past three days. He had literally turned Belleau Wood into "one huge machine-gun nest."

There was not one, but three lines of trenches running through it. The first was a little behind the southern edge and faced the villages of Lucy-le-Bocage and Bouresches. It culminated in a plateau that was a natural fortress. The plateau was scored by brush-filled ravines, was thickly wooded, and in its center was an area of enormous gray mossy boulders, the size of railroad cars, piled up and over and against one another. Major Bischoff had placed fifteen heavy Maxim machine guns among these boulders, directing their fields of fire so that if one was captured it became immediately exposed to flanking fire by another. He did not expect any of them to be captured, however, for nothing less than a series of direct hits by large-caliber shells could dislodge a man from this position.

Another line of trenches ran across the center of the wood, the narrowest part, from east to west. It was protected by lines of barbed wire, trench-mortar teams, and sharpshooters' rifle pits placed here and there to good advantage. The trees were mostly second-growth oak, elm, chestnut, and pine, and none of them was more than five or six inches thick. But they were set so closely together that, except where the major's troops had cut them down to clear a field of fire, you could not see more than ten or fifteen feet in any direction.

The third, and strongest, line of trenches ran across the northern edge of the wood. In addition to barbed wire and trench mortars, the approaches to these trenches were well-covered by German batteries behind Torcy. Just south of the trenches was a two-story hexagonal hunting lodge, the only building in the wood. It was a favorite aiming point for the artillery of both sides and, by the time the battle for the wood was over, the trophies decorating its walls—boar, deer, and fox— were obscenely riddled with shrapnel.

In all, Major Bischoff had placed nearly two hundred machine guns in the wood—more than enough, it seemed to him, to stop any ground attack the Americans might launch against him. His only weakness was the condition of his troops. The twelve hundred men under his command, veterans all, had been living for months past on a diet of black bread, barley, and dried vegetables, with an occasional piece of sausage or cheese and, of course, whatever they could forage from the countryside. Many of them were down with grippe and dysentery. Major Bischoff had repeatedly asked his superiors for better rations, but so far none had been forthcoming. Nor, he knew, were any likely to be, for food was scarce throughout Germany. But as he strolled through the wood in the stillness of late afternoon, exchanging a word with a soldier here, patting another on the shoulder there, looking from time to time across the fields that separated him from the American lines, he was confident that he had done everything possible to render his position impregnable to anything less than saturation shelling by artillery.

GERMAN observers in airplanes and balloons reported increased activity in the American lines on June 5, and during the afternoon and night their artillery sent over some two thousand shells, most of them high explosive. Just after dark one of these shells set fire to an ammunition dump near Lucy-le-Bocage and the night was rent by streams of tracers spraying in all directions. The 6th's machine-gun company was dug in nearby, and First Sergeant Dan Daly, a semilegendary leatherneck of the old school, plunged into the hell of exploding small arms with a few volunteers and put out the fire. Daly had won his first Medal of Honor at the siege of Peking in 1900; his second in Haiti in 1915; and he was recommended for a third at Vera Cruz in 1914. For putting out the fire, and for a couple of other heroic actions performed during the following week, he received a battlefield commission and was awarded the Distinguished Service Cross.

In the meantime a number of correspondents had come up from Paris to report the show. Among them was Edwin L. James of the New York *Times,* Casper Whitney of the New York *Herald Tribune,* and a chunky, energetic young man named Floyd Gibbons, who represented the Chicago *Tribune.* Gibbons had already acquired a certain renown for his work in Mexico, where he had first accompanied Pancho Villa on his campaigns against the government troops, and, later, General Pershing on his campaign against Villa. He had augmented his reputation by his brilliant account of the sinking of the liner *Laconia,* which was torpedoed off the coast of Ireland while he was aboard. Gibbons had been offered passage to Europe on a ship that was immune from submarine attack—the one that carried returning German Ambassador von Bernsdorff—but he had deliberately courted disaster in the hope of getting a story. He was a reckless, dashing fellow, impatient of criticism and somewhat of a thorn in the Army's side. One American

51

general had already tried, unsuccessfully, to have his correspondent's permit revoked because of the way he had reported a trench raid the previous January. Gibbons was fed up with the strict censorship imposed on the correspondents. "I'm sick of it," he had complained earlier to Ring Lardner. "My 'Laconia' experience has convinced me that all that is left me to do is pull some sensational stunt, and I'm going to do it. I'm going over the top with the boys at the first opportunity."

Gibbons got his chance the next day—Thursday, June 6—and his account of the action was to make "Belleau Wood" and "Marines" synonymous to the American public. It was also, thanks to an oversight on the part of the censor, to spark a bitter controversy between the Army and the Marine Corps.

CHAPTER 5

THE French 167th Division attacked on schedule at three-forty-five the following morning. Their objective was the high ground south of the Clignon River, a narrow, shallow stream that flows in a gentle semicircle north and east of Belleau Wood and touches the villages of Bussiares, Torcy, Belleau, and Bouresches. The attack was preceded by a short, intense artillery barrage. The poilus advanced well at first, driving the Germans out of several entrenched positions and starting down the road towards Bussiares. But then the fire of their own artillery, which had neglected to lengthen the range fast enough to keep pace with the advance, began falling among the infantry and causing many casualties. Under fire from both front and rear, the shaken and confused troops retreated nearly to their line of departure. Early in the afternoon they regrouped and moved out once more, but, understandably, without their initial *élan*. They were, in fact, so little confident of the future that General Harbord, visiting their sector a few days later, found them digging a system of trenches far behind the lines in preparation for a retreat.

The marines on their right—Major Turrill's battalion

of the 5th—had difficulties of their own. At three-forty-five, two companies of the battalion were spread out along an eight-hundred-yard front just northwest of Belleau Wood. The first hints of dawn were beginning to lighten the sky and, though tendrils of mist drifted here and there along the ground, it promised to be a clear, hot day. The men had stripped to their twenty-pound combat packs and were festooned with hand grenades, bandoliers of extra ammunition, and the indispensable gas masks. Their objective was a low pine-covered hill (Hill 142 on the map) about a thousand yards to the northeast, and a section of the road that ran between Torcy and Lucy-Le-Bocage. To reach the hill they would have to cross open wheat fields and meadows, little copses, and shallow ravines, all strongly held by the enemy. They were supposed to have one machine-gun battalion in support, but only half of it had arrived; and the other two companies of the battalion, which were slated to support the advance, were still in the 167th's sector. The French were to have relieved them at nine o'clock the night before, but had not yet got around to it. They did not join the attack until an hour after it had begun.

After a brief preparatory barrage by light artillery and machine guns, which did little more than alert the enemy, Major Turrill gave the order to move out and the two companies went over the top in four waves. With unconscious irony Captain John W. Thomason, Jr., a machine-gun officer of the 5th, wrote: "It was a beautiful deployment, lines all dressed and guiding true. Such matters were of deep concern to this outfit." It may have been a beautiful deployment, but it was also a deadly one. The advance in four waves was a tactic developed by the French and Germans for use in trench warfare, where only a short distance separated the front lines. Employing the sort of insane arithmetic that caused thirty million casualties in the war, they figured to lose the first three waves and gain the objective with the fourth. The costliness of this method of attack was soon brought home to the marines and they never used it again. "It was," remarked Captain Thomason, "unadapted for open warfare."

Captain George Hamilton's company, on the right, moved out into a wheat field that sloped gently upward to a square patch of trees. "We hadn't gone fifty yards," Hamilton wrote in a letter, "when they cut loose at us from the woods ahead—more machine guns than I had ever heard before."

The platoon leaders yelled "Battle sight! Fire at will!" but the marines, even the veterans, hit the ground and stayed there: the fighting in Mexico, Haiti, and Nicaragua had not prepared them for anything like this. The German heavy Maxims, firing at their full five hundred rounds per minute, literally filled the air with flying metal, and they were aimed so low that some of the marines hugging the ground—the lucky ones—had their combat packs torn to shreds on their backs. Then snipers, perched in the trees, began to pick them off, and the wounded started crying out for stretcher-bearers and first-aid men. For several minutes it seemed to Major Turrill, who was directing the action from his post of command in the jump-off trench, that the entire company would be ignominiously annihilated there in the field. He sent a runner to Major Edward Cole, who commanded the two supporting machine-gun companies, with a request for him to open fire on the woods. But the situation took a sharp change for the better before this message had time to reach Cole; for Captain Hamilton, recovering his nerve, pulled half a dozen men to their feet and led them in a wild rush on the woods. The rest of the company soon followed. Hamilton's letter continues: "From here on I don't remember clearly what happened. I have a vague recollection of urging the whole line on—faster, perhaps, than they should have gone, of grouping prisoners and sending them to the rear under one man instead of several, of snatching an Iron Cross ribbon off the first officer I got, and of shooting wildly at several rapidly retreating Boche. I carried a rifle on the whole trip and used it to good advantage. . . . Farther on we came to an open field, a wheatfield full of red poppies, and here we caught hell. Again it was a case of rushing across the open and getting into the woods. Afterwards we found out why it was they made it so hot for us. Three machine gun companies

54

were holding down these woods, and the infantry were farther back. Beside several of the heavy Maxims we later found several empty belts and a dead gunner sitting on the seat or lying nearby. . . . After going through this second wood we were really at our objective, but I was looking for an unimproved road which showed up on the map. . . . I pushed forward with the men I had with me, a platoon. I knew the rest were coming but thought they were closer. We went right down over the nose of a hill and on across an open field between two hills. Maxims were on both sides. I was pushing ahead with the automatic rifle team and didn't notice that most of the platoon had swerved off to the left to rout out the machine guns. All I knew was that there was a road ahead and that the bank gave good protection to the front. . . ."

The platoon that swerved off to the left was under Lieutenant Jonas Platt, who had joined the company just the day before. He led his men back to Hill 142, knocking out several machine guns on the way, then took command of another platoon whose leader had been killed by machine-gun fire. Platt was badly wounded in the leg a short while later, but refused to be evacuated. Instead, he dragged himself along the ground, giving the necessary orders and encouraging his men. For these actions he won the Navy Cross and the Distinguished Service Cross.

Another lieutenant in Hamilton's company found himself pinned down with an automatic rifleman behind a pile of cordwood. The Maxim that pinned them down was behind another pile of wood about thirty-five yards away. The automatic rifleman, Corporal Robert Morgan, raised up to fire a burst at the machine-gun nest. He got off one round, then slumped to his knees, mortally wounded in the head. The lieutenant took the Chauchat from his hands, waited a moment, then leaped up and emptied the clip, killing the three Germans at the machine gun.

Private John Kukoski found himself the only survivor of his squad. He worked around behind a machine gun, picked off the gunner, then charged with fixed bayonet and captured two other men and a visiting officer. He forced the Germans to carry the Maxim to the rear, where a couple of marines took it over, then escorted the prisoners personally to brigade headquarters.

Captain Hamilton went some six hundred yards beyond his objective before he decided to turn back. He was pinned down agaih and forced to crawl along a drainage ditch filled with cold water and slimy reeds. "Machine guns were just grazing my back, and our own artillery was dropping close. . . . Finally I got back and started getting the two companies together, and I sent out parties to right and left to try and hook up with French and American friends. . . ."

Some twenty-five of Hamilton's men went even farther beyond the objective than he did. A pilot-observer from Esquadrille Squadron 252 reported them fighting in the streets of Torcy. Most of them died there, overwhelmed by a full battalion of the enemy.

On Hamilton's left the other company, under Lieutenant Orlando Crowther, fared no better. They too were pinned down in the wheat by machine guns and decimated by snipers. Crowther tried to send a squad around to flank the machine gun on their left, but all eight men were cut down and killed the moment they started to move. Then a sniper's bullet hit Crowther in the throat, killing him instantly. A corporal named Geer broke the marines' temporary paralysis by leaping to his feet with a yell and charging the gun. Several other men followed him, and one of them grabbed the spitting muzzle and up-ended the Maxim on the gunner, losing his hand in the process. Geer, who was awarded the Navy Cross for his action, sent the prisoners to the rear under guard, then led the rest of the platoon forward.

The two companies—what was left of them—joined Captain Hamilton on the north slope of Hill 142 just in time to receive the first of five German couterattacks. They were helped by a platoon of engineers who had come up with Pioneer tools to entrench the position, and by the two support companies that had now joined the fight. Several of these attacks were beaten off at long range by the marines' accurate rifle fire. There were sharpshooters among them who could hit the bull's-eye three times out of five at seven hundred yards. They had, furthermore, learned to fire the Springfield '03 as fast as a G.I. in World War II could fire the semi-automatic Garand. They did this by pulling the trigger with their little finger and working the bolt with their thumb and forefinger. This marksmanship astonished the French and British, who were notoriously poor shots and, in general, considered the rifle only as something to carry a bayonet on. The Germans, however, were not surprised: their observers in the Civil War had made note of the American "squirrel-shooters' " proficiency.

The counterattacks were carried out by a battalion of the 197th Division and a battalion of the 237th. They tried to storm the slope while their artillery blasted the Americans with high explosives and forced them to keep their heads down. One of these attacks was broken up by Lieutenant Garvin, a platoon leader in one of the support companies. He led his men in a bayonet charge against a machine gun, captured it, and turned it against the enemy.

The last, and most dangerous, counterattack was stopped single-handed by Gunnery Sergeant Charles Hoffman of Captain Hamilton's company. Hoffman spotted fifteen Germans, their "coal-scuttle" helmets hugging the ground, crawling up through the bushes dragging five light machine guns. Captain Hamilton was momentarily helpless: a "potato-masher" grenade, landing nearby, had flung a stone against his temple and left him dazed. Those five machine guns, Hoffman realized, were enough to sweep the marines off the hill. He jumped to his feet with a yell and charged down the slope—alone. He bayoneted two of the Germans and, helped by several other marines who now joined him, drove off the rest, and captured the five machine guns. He himself was badly wounded, but survived. For this exploit he received the first Medal of Honor awarded the 2nd Division. . . . Hoffman had enlisted in the marines under the name of Ernest Janson in order to avoid the stigma then attached to men of German parentage and name; but after winning the Medal of Honor he reclaimed his birthright: there could no longer be the slightest doubt that he was a "good American."

In between attacks, Red Cross men on both sides

tended to the wounded, who were now lying parched and pain-racked beneath the blazing sun. Back in Major Turrill's post of command the headquarters staff could hear their cries for help drifting across the fields—"thin, pitiful voices calling out in German and English. . . . *'Ach, Himmel, hilf, hilf! Brandighe! Liebe Gott, brandighe!'* . . . 'First aid—this way—first-aid, for the love of God!' . . ." The Red Cross men worked openly at first. No one fired at them. But late in the afternoon something happened that put an end to this mutual courtesy. Several marines were watching a German first-aid team—two big men, one with a yellow beard—carry a stretcher back towards their lines. The stretcher was covered with a blanket and, at that distance, it looked as though a man were lying on it with his knees drawn up. "He's been gut-shot —poor bastard!" one of the marines commented. Just then a gust of wind flapped back one edge of the blanket and the marines could see the "poor bastard"—a heavy Maxim with several boxes of ammunition. "Thereafter," wrote Captain Thomason, "it was hard on Red Cross men and wounded: hard, in fact, on everybody. Like reasonable people, the Americans were willing to learn from the Boche. . . ; and if the Boche played the game that way—they would meet him at it."

A few days later a marine took an unmailed letter from the body of a German corporal. The letter was addressed to the corporal's father, and in it he said: "The Americans are savages. They kill everything that moves."

It was this brutal, no-quarter fighting that made the Germans at Belleau Wood call the marines *"Teufelhund"* —"Devil Dog"—a nickname that has stuck to this day.

COLONEL WISE'S battalion of the 5th had been held in reserve near La Voie du Chatel during this engagement. Soon after sunrise the walking wounded—men with bandaged heads, arms in rough slings, hobbling along with rifles for crutches—began drifting down the road towards his post of command, a farmhouse in which a dressing station had also been established. They were tired and despondent. Things had not gone at all well, they said. The Germans were too strong for them and the attack had been thrown back. They filed into the courtyard and sat down in the shade of the barn to wait until the medical corpsmen could get around to them. While waiting, they showed one another their trophies: Luger pistols, field glasses, German bayonets, and belt buckles. In another corner of the yard, silently munching black bread and sausage, was a group of wounded prisoners. Some of them were recent conscripts, boys of seventeen or eighteen, thin and pale from chronic undernourishment. "I never figured I'd be fighting kids!" one husky marine commented disgustedly.

A little later the stretcher cases began to arrive, most of them carried by German prisoners. The corpsmen gave them emergency treatment, injections of antitetanus serum or morphine (a large "T" or "M" was painted on their foreheads with iodine) and they were loaded aboard ambulances and carried to an evacuation hospital farther back. This process seemed needlessly complicated to Colonel Wise, who had been over the country earlier that day. It was a waste of time, he told Lieutenant Commander Dessai, the doctor in charge, to have the wounded carried two miles down from the village of Champillon, where the battalion aid station had been established. The road was good; the ambulances could go right up and get them. Dessai agreed to try it and, when the ambulances returned from the evacuation hospital, he sent them up towards Champillon. Just then a shell-shocked captain of engineers came down the road. He was white and trembling. The attack was a failure, he said to Colonel Wise. The marines had been cut to pieces. He stepped into the middle of the road and raised his arms to stop the ambulances from going forward. Wise grabbed him by the shoulder. "You're a damned liar! Get out of this road and leave those ambulances alone or I'll shoot you!" The captain burst into tears and resumed walking towards the rear.

Just before noon Lieutenant Colonel Richard Derby, the assistant division surgeon, (and Theodore Roosevelt's son-in-law) paid a visit to the aid station at Champillon. It was under the command of Lieutenant Richard Shea of the Navy Medical Department. "He had already passed a great many men through," wrote Colonel Derby, "and the several small rooms and shed that constituted his aid station were still crowded with wounded. . . . Shea had been sniped at that morning while standing outside his station, and showed me a hole through one of the side pockets of his blouse. . . . The closeness of this station to the front line was a fair example of the situation of the other battalion stations. . . . Our principle was, the nearer the battalion aid station to the actual scene of combat, the more quickly did the wounded man receive first aid and the sooner was his evacuation to the rear possible. . . . Where attacking troops were driving rapidly and successfully forward, this particular problem of the medical department became increasingly more difficult." It was also difficult for the medical department, as we shall see, when they had inadequate equipment, facilities, and insufficient personnel to care properly for the wounded.

General Harbord meanwhile had been anxiously trying to keep in touch with developments. Telephone communications with Major Turrill's post of command were nonexistent: by 5:00 A.M. all the wires had been cut. But a steady stream of motorcycle couriers bucketed along the shell-pocked roads and trails between brigade headquarters and the 5th Regiment headquarters with requests for up-to-the-minute information. (So many of these motorcycles were "killed in action" that a few days later, on June 11, General Bundy sent a telegram to A.E.F. Headquarters in Chaumont requesting that "fifty Indian or Harley-Davidsons be sent at once. . . . Communications seriously impaired by lack of these machines.")

At 7:30 A.M. Harbord received his first encouraging news: Lieutenant Hadrot of Esquadrille Squadron 252 reported that all the objectives had been attained. Immediately after this message was received the first prisoners were brought in to La Loge Farm and lined up in the stable yard for preliminary inspection before being escorted to the rear. Harbord went out to look them over. He was not impressed, for he found them a mangy-looking, underfed lot. There was one officer in the group, a scrawny, middle-aged man with a big mustache. He was wearing an Iron Cross around his neck and, as Harbord had never seen one before, he went up for a closer look. The German glared at him furiously. When he had completed his inspection, Harbord returned to his office and the prisoners were marched away. A few minutes later there was a knock at Harbord's door. It was a burly marine sergeant with a big grin on his face. He gave a snappy salute and held out an Iron Cross. "Sir," he said, "that officer that was wearin' this cross hopes the general will accept it."

"I have always had some doubts as to the spontaneity of the gift," Harbord wrote in his diary.

Other messages arrived later in the morning, confirming Lieutenant Hadrot's report. Hill 142 had been taken and held—but at a heavy cost. Major Turrill's battalion had lost 10 officers and 400 men, most of them in two companies. In Captain Hamilton's company alone, ninety per cent of the officers and fifty per cent of the enlisted men had been killed or wounded. It was an ominous forecast of events to come. Nevertheless the attack *had* been a success, as such things were measured, and at noon General Degoutte ordered General Bundy to put into motion the next phase—the reduction of the German salient at Lucy-le-Bocage and the capture of Belleau Wood.

CHAPTER 6

FLOYD GIBBONS decided to pull his "sensational stunt" by accompanying Major Benjamin Berry's battalion in the attack on the northern lobe of Belleau Wood at 5:00 P.M. He had already filed a skeleton dispatch to the Chicago *Tribune* with the censor in Paris. In it he praised the marines highly for their fight at Hill 142 and outlined the action in the wood—"where," he wrote, even before the battle took place, "the air seemed full of red-hot nails." Gibbons and the other reporters had obtained an important concession from the censor. Correspondents were forbidden to mention units by name or number, on the sound theory that this would give valuable information to the enemy; but they were allowed to write freely of "artillery," "engineers," "infantry," etc. Therefore, they had argued, they should also be allowed to mention "marines." After all, they pointed out, the United States Marine Corps *was* a recognized branch of the armed services. It was a delicate point, and should have been referred to General Pershing or his chief of staff, General James McAndrew, for a decision. The censor, however, took it upon himself to grant the correspondents' request, overlooking the fact that, as there was only one brigade of marines in France, mentioning them by name would amount to a unit designation.

Colonel Catlin had been ordered to direct the attack, even though one of the participating battalions—Major Berry's—was part of Colonel Neville's regiment. As things worked out, however, Catlin found it impossible to control Berry's movements, for no telephone lines had been run out to the major's post of command and it was too close to the zero hour to send messengers. So Berry's battalion conducted a virtually independent operation.

Catlin received the order to attack at 3:45 P.M. and immediately briefed Sibley and Holcomb in the latter's post of command, which was located in "Gob Gully" about five hundred yards behind the front line. His instructions, like Harbord's, were necessarily simple and straightforward: he knew too little of the enemy's dispositions to indulge in fancy tactical maneuvers.

From Holcomb's post of command, Catlin went with his French liaison officer, Captain Tribot Laspierre, through Lucy-le-Bocage to a point from which he could observe the action. On the way he passed a company of Sibley's battalion crouched in the jump-off trench waiting to go over the top. The men seemed calm and in good spirits, though rumors of Turrill's heavy losses had reached them. One of Catlin's staff suggested he make a little speech. He thought for a moment, then said simply, "Give 'em hell, boys!"

The colonel, in fact, was not at all sanguine about the chances of success in the forthcoming attack. Communications were in poor shape; Berry's men had some four hundred yards of open wheat fields to cross before they could get to close quarters with the enemy; and no one had any idea of how many Germans were holding the wood, for it had been impossible to get patrols inside it. "Sibley and Berry had a thousand men each," Catlin wrote, "but only half of these could be used for the first rush, and as Berry's position was problematical, it was Sibley's stupendous task to lead his five hundred through the southern end of the wood clear to the eastern border if the attack was not to be a total failure. Even to a marine it seemed hardly men enough."

At four-thirty the artillery and machine guns laid down a barrage on the woods. It was a hit-or-miss operation for they had no definite targets. German artillery responded—and since they had seven observation balloons floating overhead to spot targets and correct aim, their fire was more accurate and to the point. They knocked out several American batteries. Across the wheat fields and outlined against the pale blue sky, loomed the dark mass of the wood with its splintered and shell-shattered trees, its boulder-strewn plateau, and its ravines tangled with brush. "It was a moment of foreboding fit to shake nerves of steel," wrote Colonel Catlin, "like entering a dark room filled with assassins."

The officers had synchronized their watches, so there was no formal order given to attack. At exactly five o'clock a great shout rose from the American lines and a thousand men surged out of their trenches towards the woods. The New York *Times* reported the next day that the troops moved out "singing Yankee Doodle," and another newspaper said they yelled "Remember the Lusitania!" but none of the eyewitness accounts mention either of these unlikely battle cries. Several of the accounts, however, do mention a leather-lunged sergeant in Major Berry's battalion roaring: "Come on, you sons of bitches, do you want to live forever!"

It is a military axiom that the number of medals awarded after a battle is directly proportionate to the number of casualties incurred. Following the assault on June 6, Major Berry's battalion received almost a hundred Distinguished Service Crosses, Navy Crosses, Silver Stars, and Croix de Guerres. Directly affecting this number was a field order from Colonel Neville, issued two days later, which read: "The 'extraordinary heroism' which calls for the D.S.C. must be liberally interpreted in the case of officers or men who have met death or suffered the loss of a leg, an arm, or an eye in action."

Berry's men faced an impossible task. They moved out in neat, well-dressed lines with their bayonets gleaming in the sun and the smell of crushed grain rising from beneath their boots. Major Bischoff's veteran machine gunners waited until they were well out in the open before opening fire. The Maxims had been aimed just a few inches above the ground, and the marines were cut down as though by a gigantic scythe. Entire platoons were wiped out. Those who survived this first killing burst tried to advance by short rushes, but the enemy fire was too intense. Berry attempted to send a runner, Private Roy Simpson, with a message to one of his company commanders. Simpson was hit in the chest by a burst of machine-gun bullets the moment he started out. He staggered blindly forward, calling out, "I must deliver the message," and fell dead. One gunnery sergeant dragged two wounded men from in front of a machine gun and miraculously escaped unharmed; another was killed while trying to gather his scattered platoon and organize an attack; a third, First Sergeant Edmund Madsden, actually rushed to within three feet of a machine-gun nest before he was killed; still another sergeant hacked down a line of barbed wire with his bayonet and opened the way for his platoon to proceed. There were many such acts of valor, but the marines were pinned down until nightfall, when they crawled painfully back to the jump-off trench. The battalion lost over three hundred killed and wounded (sixty per cent casualties in the two assault companies), and not one man reached the woods.

Gibbons meanwhile had watched the first part of the advance from the top of a low hill some distance behind the jump-off point. He furiously scribbled notes on the back of an envelope, and asked technical questions of Lieutenant A. E. Hartzell, who had been assigned as his guide. Soon after the first waves of marines had vanished into the wheat, the two men went down and joined a machine-gun company that was preparing to advance. Gibbons asked permission to accompany it, but the company commander refused to allow him to join the "suicide club"—as machine gunners were known. It was too dangerous, he said, and besides, he was not authorized to give such permission. Gibbons and Hartzell moved further along the foot of the hill and found Major Berry. He too was preparing to move up with a machine-gun company and his headquarters staff. After some persuasion, he agreed to let Gibbons accompany him.

They filed through a little copse of pine trees and came out into a field of half-ripe oats. Major Berry was some twenty yards ahead of Gibbons and Hartzell and had just reached the middle of the field, when machine guns opened up on them from a small patch of woods on their left front. "Get down, everybody!" Berry yelled, dropping to the ground. A moment later a bullet entered his left arm at the elbow, traveled down along the bone tearing flesh and nerves, and lodged in his palm. The sudden shock and pain jerked him to his knees, and Gibbons, sprawled flat on the ground, shouted, "Get down! Flatten out, Major!"

"We've got to get forward," Berry called back presently in a voice full of pain. "They'll start shelling this open field in a few minutes."

Gibbons yelled to him to wait, that he was coming to help him. "Then we'll make a dash for it."

The correspondent began crawling forward, hugging the ground, but he had gone only a few feet when a bullet tore through the fleshy part of his upper left arm —"as though someone had touched it with a lighted cigarette." Seconds later another one seared across the top of his left shoulder. He felt no great pain and was still able to use his arm, so he continued to crawl forward, his left cheek pressed flat to the earth and his helmet cocked over his right ear. "Then there came a crash," he wrote. "It sounded to me as though someone had dropped a glass bottle into a porcelain bathtub. A barrel of whitewash tipped over and it seemed that everything in the world turned white. That was the sensation. I did not recognize it because I had often been led to believe, and often heard it said, that when one receives a blow on the head everything turns black. . . .

I did not know then that the bullet striking the ground immediately under my left cheekbone had ricocheted upward, going completely through the left eye and then crashing out through my forehead, leaving the eyeball and upper eyelid completely halved, the lower eyelid torn away, and a compound fracture of the skull. . . . Further progress toward the major was impossible. I must confess that I became so intensely interested in the weird sensations that I even neglected to call out and tell the wounded officer that I would not be able to continue. . . ."

Several minutes later, as Gibbons lay there bemused by his "weird sensations," Major Berry jumped to his feet and, clutching his left arm to his chest, made a successful dash to the woods. Before he collapsed from pain and was evacuated, he managed to direct a squad of marines in a flanking maneuver that eliminated one of the machine guns. For this action he was awarded the Distinguished Service Cross. The battalion was taken over by his second in command, Major Maurice Shearer.

Gibbons and Hartzell were pinned down in the field for three hours, unable to move without drawing fire. At nine o'clock that night they crawled back to the little copse of pines, and Gibbons, now in agony and close to death from shock and loss of blood, was given emergency treatment in an aid station and then rushed to the hospital in Paris. His "sensational stunt" cost him his left eye; from then on he wore the black patch that became, in a sense, his badge of distinction and lent a dashing, piratical air to the already glamorous figure of the foreign correspondent.

HALF an hour before Major Sibley's battalion went over the top, Lieutenant Ralph Marshall, the battalion intelligence officer, sent a four-man patrol up "Gob Gully" to see if they could locate any machine-gun nests. The patrol was led by Corporal Joseph Rendinell, a former Pittsburgh steelworker, who kept a diary that was later published under the title, *One Man's War*. Of his trip up "Gob Gully" he wrote: "So I said a little prayer. It didn't look to me like there was any chance of coming back at all. My buddies said goodbye and wished me luck and I could tell they didn't expect ever to see me again, either. I took Private Moore as the getaway man, Sleet and Private Howe to guard my flanks and keep me in sight always for any signal. If I got bumped off, Private Howe could take my place. We hunched along with our heads down. I spotted a bunch of Heinies around the bend of the ravine. I signaled to Private Moore. He rushed back to H.Q. and then the attack started. We stopped where we were until our men cleaned out that machine gun nest. I heard some shooting about fifteen feet in back of a tree and I could not see this Heinie, so I crawled out of the ravine and walked on the side, stooping real low, and then I saw him in the bushes, so I took careful aim and fired and I got me another belt buckle." (German belt buckles, with their raised inscription *"Gott Mit Uns,"* were favorite souvenirs.)

Lieutenant Marshall joined Rendinell a few minutes later and, under fire, began sending a continuous stream of information back to battalion headquarters. He won a Navy Cross and a Distinguished Service Cross for his actions in Belleau Wood on June 6. Rendinell himself was wounded the next day by gas and shrapnel, and evacuated to a base hospital in St. Agon ("Saint Agony" to the patients); but he rejoined the 6th Marines in time to take part in the final assault on the woods.

MAJOR SIBLEY'S battalion had somewhat better luck than Major Berry's, at least initially. The German defenses in the southern lobe of the wood were not as well organized as those in the north and center, and the approach was across rolling, grassy meadows that offered some cover. The marines moved out as though on parade, walking at a deliberate pace in four skirmish lines fifteen to twenty yards apart. As Colonel Catlin aptly remarked: "A man is of little use in a hand-to-hand bayonet struggle after a hundred yard dash." The first and third waves carried automatic rifles and grenades; the second and fourth, rifles. There were in addition a few men armed with sawed-off shotguns. These were remarkably efficient at close quarters—though the Germans denounced them as "barbarous."

The Germans opened up with machine guns, mortars,

and artillery, and some of Sibley's men went down, most of them with leg and belly wounds; but the rest moved steadily forward until they plunged into the woods. Colonel Catlin, despite warnings from Captain Laspierre that he was too close to the front for safety, insisted upon observing the action from a low rise about three hundred yards away. He was partially screened from view by a clump of bushes, but a machine-gun emplacement nearby was drawing enemy fire. As the first wave of marines entered the woods, the colonel took a couple of steps forward, up the rise, and raised his field glasses for a closer look at the action. Just then a sniper's bullet went through his right lung and came out beneath his shoulder blade. "It felt exactly as though someone had struck me heavily with a sledge. It swung me clear around and toppled me over on the ground. When I tried to get up I found that my right side was paralyzed."

Captain Laspierre dragged him to a shelter trench about twenty-five feet away (no easy task, for the captain was a small, slightly-built man, and Catlin a six-footer who weighed two hundred and twenty pounds), made him as comfortable as possible, and then went for help. But German artillery had found the range and, soon after he left the colonel, an exploding shell picked the captain up and flung him a dozen feet through the air. Dazed from shock and concussion, he was evacuated to an aid station.

In the meantime Catlin had been joined by other members of his staff. He sent a runner for a doctor and stretcher-bearers, and another to regimental headquarters to tell Lieutenant Colonel Harry Lee, assistant commander of the 6th, to take charge. Major Farwell, the regimental surgeon, came up with stretcher-bearers under fire and administered first aid. Both he and Catlin had to wear their gas masks, for the Germans had begun dropping high-explosive shells that contained an admixture of gas. "It was hard enough for a man to breathe with a lung full of blood," Catlin wrote, "without having one of those smothering masks clapped over his face."

Nearly two hours went by before Colonel Lee found Catlin and was brought up to date on the situation and given Sibley's latest messages. By this time the artillery barrage had slackened somewhat, so the stretcher-bearers carried Catlin to Lucy-le-Bocage, where there was a waiting ambulance that rushed him to a field hospital. He was injected with antitetanus serum and put aboard another ambulance, which carried him to Red Cross Hospital Number Two in Paris, where "quarts of blood" were drained from his pleural cavity. Later, recovering without complications, he told visitors: "Don't feel so bad about me. It's my own fault. I shouldn't have been so close to the front in a first-class war."

While Catlin was being evacuated, and Colonel Lee was trying to pick up the scattered threads of his new command, Sibley's men were engaged in a murderous fight in "Hellwood," as they came to call it. "It wasn't a battle in any recognized sense of the word," one of Sibley's officers said later. "It was an exaggerated riot." Major Bischoff's guns were placed on every slight rise in the ground, in ravines, among piles of boulders, behind stacks of cut timber, even perched in trees. They covered all zones with both lateral and plunging fire. The only effective tactic against them, the marines soon learned, was to work around behind a nest, bomb it with hand grenades, then rush forward and kill or capture the survivors. They attacked singly, in pairs, or in small groups, moving from tree to tree until close enough to throw their grenades, and then charging with lowered bayonets. Lieutenant Louis Timmerman of Company "K" led his platoon in one such charge and captured two guns and seventeen prisoners. He himself was wounded in the face by shrapnel, but remained on duty for twenty-four hours before he allowed himself to be evacuated. Private Edward Cary, who was with Timmerman in this charge, described it in a letter to his parents in St. Louis. It is less interesting as a war document than as a revelation of Cary's extreme naïveté—a naïveté that seems, from a number of other letters written by enlisted marines, to have been typical.

Cary's letter reads in part: ". . . Whooey! I never knew there were so many machine gun bullets and high explosives in the world. Two men, one on either side of me, were killed by machine gun fire, and in the fracas

69

I lost the company but hooked up with another one. A lieutenant, eight other men and myself took seventeen prisoners, three (!) machine guns, and other equipment. I had to shoot at two of them, and they fell, and, as we found them afterwards dead, I have two notches to my credit. When we came up to the Germans they threw down their arms and called 'Kamerad! Mercy!' They are as yellow as ochre and will not fight like men. As long as they are away from you they will fight, and fight damn dirty, but corner them and they quit—I could lick a squad of them with a soup ladle. . . . Some of the boys took souvenirs, but not for me. Everything they own is tainted with innocent blood and they are too damn mean and too foul to touch. The only things I have are three buttons that a young sixteen-year-old Prussian gave to me voluntarily. . . . I wasn't the least bit scared in battle."

It is quite true that many of the Germans surrendered rather than face cold steel, but a few of them grabbed up their own bayonets and fought back. Lieutenant D. B. Milner witnessed one such encounter. He saw the marine lunge twice, miss, then brain the German with his rifle butt. "I could see the veins stand out on their necks," he told a reporter afterwards. Hand-to-hand combat was the exception, however: the records of the main evacuation hospital show that only one member of the 2nd Division was admitted with a bayonet wound—and he had accidentally stabbed himself in the thigh!

The marines' difficulties were increased by the clever way Major Bischoff had set up his guns. Time after time Sibley's men took a machine-gun nest only to be pinned down by flanking fire from another. One squad, finding itself in such a predicament, left a man behind to guard the prisoners at the first gun, then worked around the flank of the second and captured it and its crew intact. In the meantime, however, the prisoners at the first gun had killed their guard and put the Maxim back into action. The marines bayoneted the crew of the second gun, then recaptured the first one and killed its crew also.

Major Berton Sibley, a short swarthy Vermonter who was affectionately known as "The Old Man" because of his quiet, studious manner, was in the thick of the fighting, leading his troops against the main German line of resistance in the southern quarter of the wood. The forty-one-year-old Sibley was remarkably cool under fire. A couple of days earlier he had been taking a nap in his hammock when a dud 150 plowed into the soft earth less than five feet away and came up with its nose directly beneath him. Sibley had looked at it for a moment, then reached down and tentatively touched its smooth snout. "Hot," he said laconically, drawing his hand away; then calmly closed his eyes and went back to sleep. But he needed all his coolness under fire to cope with the situation in the woods.

As darkness descended the scene became nightmarish, a palimpsest of yells of rage, groans, cries for first aid and water, bursts of machine-gun and rifle fire—the whole thrown into periodic relief by the ghastly greenish light of flares. The wounded dragged themselves like sick animals into patches of dense underbrush to hide until help arrived. Some of them died there and were not found until weeks or, in some cases, months later. (They were usually discovered half-eaten by "trench rabbits"—rats—or, in at least one instance, by pigs that had run wild.) Stretcher-bearers and combat patrols roamed about in the darkness, occasionally encountering their enemy counterparts, for the marines did not hold a continuous line, only isolated strongpoints connected by patrols and machine guns laid for interlocking fire. There were wild alarms and hysterical outbursts of rifle and machine-gun fire when these groups met. Liaison was impossible to maintain, and the men found themselves in different platoons and companies from those in which they had started out.

During this initial phase of the attack Sibley had reported either to the regimental adjutant, Major Evans, or directly to General Harbord, for he was unable to locate Colonel Lee. Harbord, indeed, was unhappy with Lee's performance and sent him the following blistering message: "I am not satisfied with the way you have conducted your engagement this afternoon. Your own Regimental Headquarters and this office have not had a word of report from you as to your orders or your positions. Major Sibley under your command is asking your regimental adjutant for orders. Major Berry [at the time he sent this message Harbord had not yet been informed that Berry was wounded] over whom you should have asserted your authority, is reporting to his own regimental commander. I want you to take charge and push this attack with vigor. Carry the attack through the woods. . . . and send Sibley to take Bouresches. Holcomb is instructed to advance his line to conform to the movement. . . . I want reports from you every fifteen minutes. Send them by runner if necessary. Major Sibley has had telephone connection with your Regimental Headquarters all afternoon." In justice to Colonel Lee, it must be said that he had had great difficulty in finding Colonel Catlin after he was wounded, and an equally hard time, in the confusion of battle, establishing liaison with his battalion commanders.

Finally, at about nine o'clock, Sibley and the survivors of his two companies (less than half of the original five hundred men) were held up by the boulder-strewn plateau where Major Bischoff had placed fifteen machine guns. They had reached their first objective—the edge of the woods—and had gained a precarious toe hold along the southern and eastern strips; but they could make no further progress until Stokes mortars were brought up and the supply of hand grenades replenished. Two companies of engineers came up from Lucy-le-Bocage to help the marines entrench their position, and Sibley passed the word down the line to dig in and make no further attempt to advance until daybreak.

MAJOR HOLCOMB'S battalion of the 6th, on Sibley's right, had been ordered to keep pace with the advance and maintain contact with the left of the 23rd Infantry. After Colonel Catlin had briefed him in his post of command, Holcomb ordered two companies to move up to the jump-off line. One of these companies passed through a cluster of farmhouses called Montgivrault Grand, and some of the marines went into the houses to look for food or drink. They found nothing; the retreating French had stripped the village clean. But in one of the houses they were surprised to find an old couple, both past seventy, who had refused to leave when the Germans were advancing. They were gaunt with hunger, so the marines left a few cans of beef and some hardtack with them. A few days later, on their way back from the front, these same marines passed through Montgivrault Grand again, and they stopped in to see how the old folks were getting along. The old man had disappeared—no one knew where. But they found the old woman in the barn. She had hanged herself from a rafter with a length of ribbon. . . .

Sibley's second objective had been the village of Bouresches, about three-quarters of a mile east of the southern lobe of Belleau Wood. It soon became apparent that he had all he could handle in the woods, so Holcomb's Company H under Captain Donald Duncan undertook to capture it. This happened by accident rather than by design, for Duncan never received a formal order to attack the village. His men, moving ahead and trying to keep in touch with the troops on both flanks, found themselves confronted by the red-roofed houses of Bouresches, about five hundred yards away and just beyond a shallow, grassy valley. So they kept pushing forward—into a fierce machine-gun and artillery barrage from both flanks and from the village, which was defended by a battalion of the German 10th Division.

Captain Duncan, an empty pipe clenched tightly in his jaws, a swagger stick swinging from his left hand and an automatic from his right, led half the company. The other half was under Lieutenant James Robertson, one of his platoon commanders. Robertson's men made faster progress through the valley, though they lost heavily, and when the lieutenant topped the rise on the far side, he turned back for a moment to see how the rest of the company was managing. He saw them racing through the barrage, Duncan at their head, and "going down like flies." Then he turned away and, with the twenty men still on their feet (out of more than a hundred who had entered the valley with him), plunged into the village.

Duncan was hit in the mouth by machine-gun bullets a few seconds later. Dental Surgeon Weedon Osborne, who had joined the regiment just a few days before, and an aid man, picked him up and started back across the valley towards a dressing station. A direct hit from an 88 killed all three of them before they got there. The rest of Duncan's men joined Robertson in Bouresches and began a savage house-to-house fight for possession of the village.

The Germans had set up machine guns on the roofs and in the cellars, behind barricades and at blind corners. Each one was protected by a squad of riflemen. Robertson's orderly, Private Herbert Dunlavy, single-handedly attacked and captured one of the Maxims (he himself was killed the following night), and Private Earl Belfry, though wounded, led a successfull assault on another. Holcomb sent in Lieutenant Wallace Leonard with forty-three men to reinforce Robertson. They tried to avoid the valley, which was still under intense fire, and enter the village by way of a path that wound around from the south. But they were caught in a triangular nest of at least six machine guns. Leonard led a wild charge with rifles and bayonets and killed the crews of several guns. When the mêlée was over he had four men left, and there were three bullet holes through his uniform.

An erroneous report reached Harbord that Holcomb's men had not only taken Bouresches but the railroad embankment beyond it as well. Encouraged by this news, Harbord telephoned Colonel Brown at division headquarters and said he was prepared to increase the scope of the attack by committing three reserve companies that were near Lucy-le-Bocage. "But I will have to know in advance if I can depend on any other source if I get in trouble," he told the colonel.

"We'll back you up," Brown replied.

Harbord abandoned this plan, however, when he received a message from Holcomb giving the true situation. "Lieutenant Robertson holds the east edge of Bouresches," the message read. "Enemy holds the station and railroad embankment. I have sent in one platoon as reinforcements. Robertson says Belleau Wood is held by the enemy. Unless Sibley can do something in way of taking left part of the objective, we are in a hole. We also need reinforcements to hold our line of resistance."

Shortly after this message was received at brigade headquarters at 11:20 P.M., a wounded runner staggered into Holcomb's post of command with an urgent message from Robertson. The lieutenant and his men were almost out of ammunition, the runner said, and the enemy was starting to counterattack. Unless help reached them soon, they risked being wiped out.

The situation was saved by Lieutenant William Moore and Sergeant Major John Quick, who volunteered to drive a truckload of ammunition into Bouresches. Moore, a good-looking young man who went to war with a German police dog named Straff, had been president of the senior class, captain of the track team, and star halfback at Princeton the year before. Quick was a veteran of thirty years' service with the Corps, another semilegendary leatherneck of the same stamp as Dan Daly. He had won the Medal of Honor in 1898 by signaling the fleet from an exposed hilltop near Guantanamo Bay, Cuba; and in 1914 he had hoisted the Stars and Stripes above the Hotel Terminal in Vera Cruz. "I think he must carry a rabbit's foot or some other amulet about with him," wrote Colonel Catlin, "for he has repeatedly risked his life in the most hazardous undertakings and he has usually come through without a scratch. . . . They say the only time he ever got hurt was at the end of a long march in the Philippines to rescue a detachment of Americans who had been cut off. Nearly dead with exhaustion and hunger, he fell over a precipice into a river. A native pulled him out and he spent the next two months in the hospital. . . ."

Both Moore and Quick won the Distinguished Service Cross for their wild night ride along a rutted and shell-pocked road into Bouresches with the vital ammunition, while machine guns and "whiz-bangs" peppered the body of the truck with bullets and shrapnel. Then Holcomb sent in another company, under Captain Randolph Zane (killed the following October), and Sibley rushed in his two support companies. The marines proceeded to clean the Germans out of the rest of the village, but they were unable to take the railroad station and embankment, for the Germans launched a series of savage counterattacks that kept them fully occupied for the rest of the night.

Another wild ride was taken that night, this one by Private Morris Fleitz in the panel truck known as "Elizabeth Ford." "Lizzie" had been presented to the 6th Regiment by Mrs. Elizabeth Pearce of New York City. The Ford was used as an ambulance when the regiment was in Bordeaux, then as a mail-and-rations carrier when the marines spent a short spell in the trenches near Verdun, relieving French troops for the fighting before Amiens. In Verdun she crashed into a ditch and lost her top. But it was at Belleau Wood and Bouresches that "Lizzie" rose to the heights of her fame. "Later in the night," wrote Major Evans in another letter to Major General Barnett, "we sent the Ford out with rations. For the next five days she made that trip day and night, and for one period ran almost every hour for thirty-six hours. She not only carried ammunition up to the men who were less than two hundred yards from the Boche [in Bouresches] but rations and pyrotechnics, and then, to the battalion on the left of the road, in those evil Belleau Woods, she carried the same, and water, which was scarce there. For these trips she had to stop on the road, and the stores were then carried by hand to a ravine ["Gob Gully"]. I saw her just after her first trip and counted twelve holes made by machine guns and shrapnel. At one time the driver, Private Fleitz, and his two understudies, Haller and Bonneville, had to stop to make minor repairs. Another time, when she had a blowout, how she and the men escaped being annihilated is a mystery. The last time I saw her she was resting against a stone wall in the little square of Lucy-le-Bocage—a shell-wrecked town—and she was the most battered object in the town. One tire had been shot off; another wheel hit; her radiator hit; and there were not less than forty hits on her. We are trying in every possible way to find new parts and make a new Ford of her. She is our Joan of Arc and if it takes six old cars to make her run again, we'll get those six and rob them. The men have a positive and deep-seated affection for her that is touching."

Shortly after Major Evans wrote this letter, Private Fleitz painted a Croix de Guerre on the Ford's hood. And Wallace Irwin wrote a long poem in her honor, the final refrain of which goes:

Cute little 'Lizabeth, dear little 'Lizabeth,
    Bonnie Elizabeth Ford!
Where shrapnel has mauled her we've now overhauled her,

Her wheels and gears restored.
Her record's clean, she's a true Marine
And we're sending the Dutch War Lord
A note by Elizabeth, chunky Elizabeth,
Spunky Elizabeth Ford!

Colonel Wise's battalion (less Captain Lloyd Williams' company, which had been temporarily assigned to Major Turrill) was held in reserve along the northern edge of Belleau Wood while Sibley's and Holcomb's men were fighting in the woods and the village. At midnight a runner arrived with orders—"the damndest I ever got in my life," Wise wrote later. "It went on the calm assumption that all the objectives of Turrill's and Berry's battalions had been secured. Starting at 2:00 A.M. I was to go along the road between Lucy-le-Bocage and Torcy, find Colonel Feland [Lieutenant Colonel Logan Feland, Assistant Commander of the 5th Marines] whose post of command was somewhere near Champillon, and get orders."

Wise sent runners to tell Feland he was on his way, but they returned shortly saying they had been unable to find him. It was a black, moonless night and Wise had only a rudimentary map to guide him. He had kept somewhat abreast of the situation: he knew, for example, that Turrill's battalion had been successful and that Berry's had not, but he did not know the extent of either the success or the failure. He assembled his troops with some difficulty, for the enemy had shelled the area a short while before and the men had dispersed widely in their search for shelter. Promptly at two o'clock, however, he started down the road, which ran between high banks—"like the neck of a bottle"—for about half a mile and then opened out into wide wheat fields.

To the south the sky was lit by flashes of artillery and the men could hear, muffled by the intervening forest, the booming of the heavy guns and the staccato music of rifles and machine guns. They had marched along steadily, silently, for perhaps twenty minutes when Wise "got a hunch" and passed the word down the line to halt. Taking Lieutenant Legendre and two squads from the headquarters company, he went ahead to reconnoitre. About

77

two hundred yards further along the road, just before it opened out into the fields, his hunch was borne out: rifles opened up on him from the left and some of his men went down. The rifles, Wise could tell from their sound, were Springfields. "What the hell do you mean by shooting into us!" he yelled. "We're Americans!"

The firing stopped and voices called out, identifying themselves as survivors of Berry's battalion. "Look out!" they cried. "The Germans are on your right!"

Wise and his men began running back the way they had come, but had covered less than twenty yards when the Germans opened fire from the edge of the woods. Sparks flew at the marines' feet, for this section of the road was metaled and had chunks of rock in it, and many of the men went down with leg and belly wounds. Lieutenant Legendre later won the Navy Cross by crawling back up the road under fire and dragging two wounded men—the only two still alive—back to safety.

Wise's hunch had spared the battalion many casualties. He called his company commanders forward and told them: "Those damned woods on our right are full of Germans. We'll take up the ridge on our left. It looks as though what's left of the Third Battalion [Berry's] is there."

As the marines began to disperse along the ridge, German snipers opened fire. Captain John Blanchfield, standing a few feet from Wise, clutched at his groin and then doubled up and fell. A couple of his men picked him up, but he was dead before they got him behind the ridge. Other officers and men went down before the bulk of the battalion reached cover. A hot fire-fight developed, first with rifles and machine guns, then, when the Germans informed their batteries behind Torcy of the Americans' positions, with artillery and heavy mortars. Wise, moving along behind the ridge, found fifty men of Berry's battalion—all that remained of a company of two hundred and fifty—and incorporated them into his command. At first the marines alternately dug foxholes in the sandy soil and exchanged fire with the enemy in the woods across the road. But when the artillery began to land among them, they put aside their weapons and concentrated on digging in. "Everywhere up and down the

78

line," wrote Colonel Wise, "masses of earth, trees, chunks of rock, leaped into the air as the shells exploded."

Shortly after daybreak Colonel Feland came up behind the ridge on foot. Turrill's battalion, he said, was a little on the left, but the rest of Berry's had been taken out of the line and was now in reserve near Lucy-le-Bocage. He told Wise to hold the ridge until further orders, then returned to his post of command.

THE infantry brigade, under Brigadier General Edward Lewis, had been assigned a minor role in the day's operations: it was merely to "conform" to the advance of Major Holcomb's battalion on the left. Nevertheless they managed to botch the operation thoroughly.

Two battalions of the 23rd were to advance a short distance to "prevent a re-entrant angle in the line." Early in the afternoon, after receiving these orders from General Lewis, the regimental commander, Colonel Paul Malone, personally visited the two battalion posts of command and with a red pencil marked out the new positions on the map. This map saved the colonel from the disgrace of being relieved of his command, for it was sent along to division headquarters when an investigation was made two days later, and clearly supported his contention that he had given the correct orders to the battalion commanders. Major Waddill, commanding the battalion on the left, understood the orders: he was not to move forward until the marines on his left did. But Major Charles Elliott, on Waddill's right, somehow got the idea that the advance was unconditional, and at five o'clock ordered his troops to move out in a general advance. Waddill's men, obliged to protect the left of Elliott's battalion, were sucked along willy-nilly, and the two battalions, without artillery or machine-gun support, found themselves engaged in a fierce battle with a regiment of the German 10th Division, which held Bouresches and the line south of it.

Elliott's battalion suffered heavily from machine guns that took them on the flank. One company lost a hundred and forty men, and a report reached division headquarters that another company had been completely wiped out.

This was not quite true, however, as General Lewis's intelligence officer pointed out in a message that he sent to Colonel Brown the following morning: "Report saying one company of 23rd wiped out is erroneous. Only about fifty per cent wiped out. Commanding officer and several men fought all night and got back this morning."

The unfortunate tangle was compounded by a young engineer officer who, arriving with an entrenching detachment and seeing the fields ahead of him strewn with dead and wounded Americans, sent a panicky message saying that the Germans had broken through and the regiment was in dire straits. This message was forwarded to Colonel Malone and General Lewis, who at once ordered the regimental and brigade reserves into the breach. Lewis then investigated, learned how the rumor had started, and telephoned General Bundy that all was well. (But the regimental and brigade reserves still lost an all-important night's sleep.)

The mess was finally straightened out and Waddill's and Elliott's battalions retreated to the positions they had originally been told to occupy. Elliott's "misunderstanding" cost the regiment two hundred and fifty-two casualties. Early the next morning Major Waddill sent him a message: "We are going to bury Lieutenant Mathis and the other dead of our battalion at dusk tonight. Don't you want to get together with me and have a 23rd Infantry cemetery?" Elliott in turn sent a message to his company commanders: "The Boche fired on volunteer litter-bearing detail which went out to recover bodies of dead American soldiers; therefore, shoot every Boche seen on our front."

Elliott was reprimanded, but no disciplinary action was taken against him. "It is not deemed best," General Lewis wrote to General Bundy, "to curb the fine offensive spirit shown. . . ."

SHORTLY before midnight on June 6 Colonel Derby, the assistant division surgeon, led a small convoy of ambulances to Major Holcomb's aid station, which was located in a farmhouse in Petit Montgivrault, just off the Paris-Metz highway. "The collection of farmhouses and barns . . . were under fire at the time," he wrote, "and as

I stepped from the car and turned up a hedge-lined lane leading to the dressing station, I felt the combined rush and explosion of a shell, which toppled me over against the hedge, and on top of me a mule drawing a machine gun cart. The orderly of the Ford ambulance was killed and the driver of another car wounded by the same shell. The mule was between them and me. In the dust . . . and the pitch blackness, I groped my way to the wounded driver, guided by his groans. With the assistance of an ambulance driver, who turned up out of the darkness, I got the wounded man on a stretcher, and together we stumbled with him to the aid station. . . . Passing through several overlapping ponchos hung in the doorway to conceal the interior lighting, I was at first blinded . . . by the bright candlelight from within. The small room was the scene of intense activity. Two litter racks occupied the central floor space, each supporting a wounded man who was being worked over by a medical officer and several hospital corpsmen. Clamps had just been applied to a divided brachial artery in a badly wounded upper arm, and the tourniquet was being loosened but left in place to guard against accident during his subsequent evacuation. Major Farwell, the surgeon . . . was exhausted, and his second in command, Captain Boone, was directing the dressings and evacuations with great speed and skill. As soon as the wounded were dressed and cared for, they were taken down to an adjoining cellar, where they awaited the arrival of an ambulance. With shells hissing close to the roof, and only a thin wall between this roomful and the enemy's guns, this was a particularly dangerous station. Several days later the building received a direct hit, and the ceiling and roof collapsed upon this same room burying ten or twelve men and killing a number of them. About seven hundred and fifty wounded had been passed through this one station during the preceding thirty-six hours, and in the flickering candlelight the doctors and their assistants looked worn and haggard from their hard work and the terrible strain under which it had been accomplished. Having exhausted their strength, they worked on their nerves, automatically doing what instinct dictated. These were days in which men worked until they dropped and then rose to work again. Human strength was tested to the breaking point, and yet there was work to do."

There was indeed work to do. On June 6 the marine brigade alone lost almost eleven hundred men and gained only a small fraction of its objective. Nor did they inflict compensatory punishment on the enemy, for the Germans in Belleau Wood and Bouresches lost a combined total of 431 men, and they still held four-fifths of the wood, as well as the railroad station and embankment beyond Bouresches. And, as General Harbord wrote later: "More than Belleau Wood was at stake, more than standing between the invader and Paris. It was a struggle for psychological mastery. . . . The stage was small—but the audience was the world of 1918."

CHAPTER 7

THE best way to understand the medical situation is to follow a wounded man through the mill, from battlefield to base hospital. Call him George Anderson, a private in Major Sibley's battalion. Say he is twenty-two years old (the average age of the enlisted marine) and from the Middle West, perhaps Ohio or Illinois. Say a 77-millimeter "whiz-bang" exploded near him shortly after he entered the woods on the evening of June 6 and he received a typical "bottle wound" in the right thigh—a deep, jagged lesion containing a piece of shrapnel, cloth, bone fragments, and dirt. His buddies have dragged him to relative shelter behind a tree, wished him luck, and moved on. He has applied his first-aid pack to the wound but can not walk to the battalion dressing station, for his leg is broken. There are other men lying nearby, some dead, some wounded. The wounded are crying out for help or water, or groaning in agony. Their cries increase his fear and confusion; he is suddenly acutely aware that he is in a foreign land, and helpless. Will he be left here to die in this God-forsaken place? He soon adds his voice to theirs, calling out hoarsely "First aid—oh, God! —first aid!" The sanitary men hear him but there are so many wounded to be picked up that a full hour passes before a team of litter-bearers come along and carry him to the dressing station, which is located beneath a stone culvert in "Gob Gully."

In the dressing station there is another long wait, for there are many men whose wounds are critical and demand precedence—men with arms or legs blown off, men with jaws shot away, men with gaping holes in their abdomens or machine-gun bullets stitched neatly across their chests. Propped against the damp stone wall of the culvert, with the clamor of combat only a few hundred yards away, Anderson watches the doctor, his hands and forearms red with blood, go about his work. He sees things he will never forget.

Eventually the doctor finds time for him. He slits his trousers with a pair of scissors, gives the wound a cursory examination, then paints it with iodine and covers it with a sterile bandage. A pat on the shoulder, a brisk "You'll be all right, lad," and he moves on to the next man. Sanitary men place Anderson's leg in a splint from ankle to groin but do not set the bone. They tie a linen tag through a buttonhole in his shirt: on it is written his name, serial number, company, and the treatment he has received. Then they give him a shot of antitetanus serum, paint a large "T" on his forehead with iodine, and carry him to a collecting point on the road to wait his turn for evacuation.

Some time passes before he is evacuated, for the division has only forty-one ambulances (not counting nineteen mule-drawn vehicles which were of very limited use). Three U.S. ambulance sections, comprising an additional sixty vehicles, were attached to the division that morning, but even these are far from enough to handle all the wounded, and trucks and touring cars have been pressed into service as well.

It is after midnight when Anderson is finally put on a stretcher and placed in the back of a Ford ambulance with three other wounded men. The nearest hospital— American Red Cross Hospital Number Six—is in the village of Juilly, near Meaux, over thirty-five miles behind the lines. The road is in terrible condition, full of shell holes and ruts, and the driver has to proceed without lights against a stream of trucks, ambulances, motor-cycles with and without sidecars, a variety of mule-drawn vehicles, and men on foot, and with the additional hazard of periodic enemy shelling thrown in for good measure. It is a dot-and-go-one process and, provided the ambulance does not break down or get riddled with shrapnel, he is lucky to average five miles an hour.

The trip is torture for the men in the back of the ambulance. The initial shock has worn off and their wounds are very painful. Each bump brings an involuntary cry of agony from their lips. Most likely they are too immersed in their own misery to wonder why the nearest hospital is so far away, and why it is taking them so long to get there, and why the medical department is so short-handed that there is no attendant to ride with them.

It is full daylight, from twelve to sixteen hours after Anderson was wounded, when the ambulance clatters through the village, past the church, and enters a large white gateway with the American flag waving above it. It proceeds along a cobbled drive to a group of weather-worn buildings of massive construction. Beyond them is a little lake on which swans are swimming, and handsome trees with statues set here and there among them. The building on the right of the drive, the largest of the group, has a Virgin and Child on the peak of the gable. The Child's arms are outstretched in the form of the Cross. Next to the building, in sharp contrast to the smooth expanse of lawn on which it lies, is an untidy heap of bloody bandages and the festering débris of the operating room. The ambulance turns sharply to the right, around the building, and enters a flagstoned courtyard—the *Cours d'Honneur*—and stops before a huge tent. Anderson has arrived at the Collège de Juilly, a twelfth-century boys' boarding school that has been converted into an evacuation hospital.

The Collège is in a state of unparalleled confusion, for it was never intended to cope with the flood of wounded now pouring into it. While Ford ambulances stream in from Belleau Wood and Château-Thierry, General Motors ambulances, each one carrying six post-operative wounded, race back towards the larger hospitals in Paris.

(The Fords were favored for front-line work because of their ruggedness and shorter turning circle.) Trucks roll in through the gate with equipment and personnel. The arriving men have no time even to find quarters. They dump their gear on the lawn and are immediately set to work—raising tents, digging graves, carrying amputated limbs to the incinerator, replacing exhausted litter-bearers and orderlies, assisting the doctors and nurses in a hundred different ways.

According to the agreement between Pershing and Foch, the French were supposed to evacuate and hospitalize all Americans who were wounded while serving with the Sixth French Army. But when the Germans overran the Chemin des Dames they captured hospitals containing a total of forty-five thousand beds, as well as enormous quantities of equipment and supplies, and the French found themselves unable to live up to their end of the agreement. Indeed, they had not enough beds left to accommodate their own sick, much less the wounded of a foreign army. General Duchesne, however, did not inform the Americans of this state of affairs until June 2, when the 2nd Division was already sustaining casualties. General Ireland, chief surgeon of the A.E.F., made a hurried survey and learned that the Collège de Juilly was the only American institution available for service as an evacuation hospital. It was run by the Red Cross, an independent organization, and had a capacity of two hundred and fifty beds. It was staffed by two surgeons and a handful of nurses, orderlies, and Annamite litter-bearers. Since General Ireland's survey, its capacity has been increased to eight hundred beds, and surgeons, Army and Red Cross nurses, attendants, and equipment and supplies have been rushed there from all over France. The personnel of Evacuation Hospital Number Eight—the only such unit available in France (thanks to General Foch's insistence that only infantry and machine-gun units be sent from the States)—are on their way, but because the French have bungled their transportation they will not arrive until June 8. The chief medical officer of the 2nd Division has sent a detachment of men to aid the litter-bearers, and, by sending frantic telegrams to every American base hospital, has rounded up additional teams of surgeons. But these last-minute arrangements are far from adequate.

On June 6 and 7 more than one thousand seven hundred wounded are admitted to the Collège. The surgeons perform more major operations *each day* than civilian surgeons perform in six months. They have been working twenty hours a day since June 2 and are close to collapse. Their work, naturally, has been affected and they have undoubtedly made mistakes, some of them fatal, which they would not have made had conditions been better. The litter-bearers—most of them French soldiers unfit for duty at the front—have worked even longer hours; some of them are so tired that they can no longer lift a stretcher to the second tier of an ambulance.

Anderson, of course, is unaware of these conditions. A couple of men lift him out of the ambulance, carry him inside the building, and lay him on the floor alongside the other recently arrived wounded. They remove the splint and take off his uniform, cutting the trousers so that he does not have to bend his leg; put his personal possessions in a cloth bag and write his name and serial number on it with indelible ink; slip a hospital shift on him; then cover him with a blanket and carry him up a broad flight of stairs to the X-ray and fluoroscope room on the second floor.

The technician in charge of the room looks at his wound through the fluoroscope and draws two lines on his leg with silver nitrate, one on top and one on the side. Where perpendicular bisectors of these lines would meet within the thigh, the surgeon will find the shrapnel. Then Anderson is carried out to the corridor and set down on the tile floor at the end of a long line of men waiting their turn in the operating room.

One by one the wounded are carried through the door at the far end of the corridor, and one by one, from fifteen minutes to two hours later, they are carried out again. They breathe deeply and heavily, are soaked with sweat, and bear with them the sickening sweet smell of ether. Some of them do not breathe at all: their faces are covered and they sway from side to side as the litter-bearers carry them to the morgue, a white tent on the lawn outside.

Finally it is Anderson's turn. He is momentarily blinded by the dazzling whiteness of the operating room. It is about fifteen feet square and has three linoleum-covered tables in the center. Around two of the tables masked, white-gowned figures are bending over their work; the third table is empty, and an orderly is swabbing up a pool of blood that has collected at the lower end. Against the wall on his left Anderson sees an oil stove with a gleaming copper tank on top of it. The tank is a primitive autoclave, used for sterilizing the instruments, and plumes of steam are rising from it. Against the wall facing him, between two windows, is a wooden table covered with a sheet on which row after row of highly polished instruments are arrayed. On his right there are several enamel basins at which the surgical team—two surgeons and a nurse—are busy scrubbing their hands and forearms.

Anderson is lifted to the operating table and tied down with two broad canvas straps, one above his knees and the other around his chest. An orderly cuts off the bandage that was put on his leg in the battalion dressing station, then shaves the area around the wound and paints it liberally with iodine. The surgeons have finished scrubbing up and are putting on sterile gowns and rubber gloves. The actual operation will be performed by Doctor John H. Long of Navy Base Hospital Number One in Brest.

The anesthetist, an Army nurse, sits on a low stool at the head of the table. Her equipment consists of cans of ether, a mask, vaseline, gauze, a kidney-shaped basin, and clips to pull the patient's tongue forward in case he should start to choke. She looks inquiringly at Doctor Long, who nods in reply. She smears vaseline around Anderson's eyes to prevent ether burns and give the mask a tight seal, holds the mask just above his face, and begins to pour ether onto it. "Count to twenty—slowly," she says. A moment later she lowers the mask against his face and wraps a piece of gauze around the edge so that the fumes cannot escape. Anderson groans, struggles briefly, and then goes under. The operation begins.

Anderson's greatest danger is not from the wound itself but from *bacillus aerogenes capsulatus,* more commonly known as "gas gangrene." Virtually every wounded man, especially those with "bottle wounds" caused by shrapnel, is infected by it to some degree. The germ, which was isolated before the war by Doctor William H. Welch of Johns Hopkins, is anaerobic—that is, it lives only in the absence of air—and it flourishes particularly well in soil that has been fertilized with animal manure, such as is found all over France. Carried inside the body by a jagged piece of metal, it multiplies at a furious rate, breaking down the sugar of the tissues and producing large amounts of carbon dioxide gas which collects in bubbles beneath the skin. These bubbles move and crackle almost as if they were alive. Indeed, in a sense they are alive, for they shut off circulation and allow various putrefactive organisms to attack the tissues. It is these organisms that give off the characteristic stench associated with gas gangrene. The infection spreads so rapidly that it is not uncommon for a man to die within fifteen hours after he has been wounded—and Anderson, you will remember, has been waiting longer than that to be operated on.

During the Civil War nearly fourteen out of every hundred wounded died in the hospital. Most of these deaths were caused by "hospital gangrene," as it was then called. The hospitals themselves were the breeding grounds of the infection. Aided by staphylococci and streptococci, which used up the oxygen and allowed the bacillus to multiply, gas gangrene killed with plague-like rapidity. During the First World War, however, because of improved techniques developed primarily by French surgeons in 1915, only eight out of every hundred wounded died in the hospital. . . . Doctor Long is now employing these new techniques on Anderson.

An uninformed observer would be horrified by the seemingly careless abandon with which the doctor wields his scalpel. At the beginning of the operation the wound is, say, one inch long and three inches deep. When Doctor Long finishes cutting, it is seven inches long, three inches wide, and four inches deep—a gaping hole big enough to hide a billiard ball. This technique is known as "debridement," and calls for cutting away freely in all directions until nothing but healthy muscle is exposed and—theoretically, at least—all sites of possible infection have been removed. It leaves enormous scars, and occasionally the doctor is required to remove so much of the "belly" of the muscle that the limb will be useless thereafter; but it saves lives.

Doctor Long does not close the wound when he has finished cutting. He puts into practice the Carrel-Dakin method (named after Doctor Alexis Carrel, the famed Franco-American surgeon, and British scientist Doctor Henry Dakin), placing a number of thin rubber tubes into the wound, working them into every crevice where infection might lurk, then packing the hole with gauze that has been soaked in Dakin solution.

Dakin solution is a simple disinfectant composed of chlorinated lime, sodium carbonate, boric acid, and water. It is a slight modification of Javel water, which has been used as a bleaching agent and disinfectant for well over a century. The modification, though slight, is very important. Hypochlorite solutions normally corrode human tissue: Doctor Dakin learned how to neutralize this effect without destroying the solution's germ-killing powers.

Every two hours Dakin solution will be pumped through the rubber tubes into the wound; cultures will be taken daily and analyzed in the laboratory. When the bacterial count shows that the antiseptic has completely destroyed every last trace of infection, Anderson will be taken once more to the operating room and his wound will be closed with sutures. This, however, will not be done in Juilly, for Anderson is not one of the "nontransportable" wounded. In a day or two he will be taken to a Red Cross hospital in Paris, and from there, a couple of days later, to a base hospital in southwestern France. Nontransportable wounded are those with sucking chest wounds, perforating abdominal wounds, or severe haemorrhages. Later, when the medical department is better organized, the nontransportables will be held in field hospitals a couple of thousand yards behind the front lines. These field hospitals, however, will not be operating until

June 9. In the meantime, the nontransportables have already been transported more than thirty-five miles, a trip that many of them did not survive.

Anderson, then, is one of the luckier wounded: he has no massive gas infection and in time will recover the full use of his leg. Here is the hospital form, by no means unusual, of the marine who was not so lucky:

June 7, 1918. 1:30 A.M.   Ward B
M——, H—— T.   Serial No. 12220674
Corporal, Machine Gun Co. 5th Marines
Duration of injury, 11 hours.

    I. G.S.W. (Gun Shot Wound) right thigh, perforating, involving knee joint. Complicated by gas infection. Debridement about half the extensor muscles of thigh. Wound of entrance and exit in knee joint debrided, joint irrigated with ether, capsule closed with chromic gut. 8 C.D. tubes (Carrel-Dakin tubes).

    II. G.S.W. lateral aspect right buttock, extensive areas of skin and fascia lost. Debridement. 6 C.D. tubes.

    III. G.S.W. right leg, perforating F.C.C. (compound comminuted fracture) tibia middle and lower third, extensive loss of bone substance. Anterior tibial vessels severed. Debridement. 5 C.D. tubes.

    IV. G.S.W. right calf, outer side. Small éclat (fragment of shrapnel) removed. Dakin dressing.

    V. G.S.W. middle right leg. Small éclat removed. Slight notch in anterior of tibia. Debridement. 1 C.D. tube.

    VI. G.S.W. right hand Iodine dressing.
Hold.   Capt. Long (signed)

Infection lingered in Corporal M——'s right leg, despite further operations, and three weeks later it was amputated. He died on the operating table and was buried the next evening in the village cemetery, along with five other men who had died the same day. Frederick Pottle, the well-known scholar and editor, who was then an orderly in Evacuation Hospital Number Eight, described the burial. "We piled them into a high two-wheeled cart, drawn by a great patient work horse, and spread out an American flag over the ends of the boxes. The little procession started from the *Cours d'Honneur,* at the head the little crucifer from the parish church, then our Y.M.C.A. chaplain in his plain khaki uniform, walking side by side with the village curé in his biretta, cassock, surplice, and stole. Behind trudged a French urchin, bearing the pail of holy water, a cotta over his breeches, but with American trench cap on his head. Then came the lumbering cart driven by its stolid French owner, and, walking beside it, the men of the burial detail. At the cemetery we unloaded the coffins and lowered them down into the graves, jumping impatiently on the tops of the boxes if they happened to stick in the narrow space, and then stood uncovered, leaning on our spades, as the curé in his clear sonorous voice read the grand Latin of the Roman burial service over Catholic, Protestant, Jew, and Gentile, and our chaplain followed with the familiar English words. One sprinkled with holy water, the other cast in a handful of earth. The bugler . . . blew the tender notes of taps. . . ."

CASPER WHITNEY, the correspondent for the New York *Herald Tribune,* was not as flamboyant as his colleague, Floyd Gibbons. He had no desire to "go over the top with the boys." But he was a good reporter nevertheless: inquisitive, skeptical, thorough. He became interested in the medical aspects of the war and decided to look into them. He visited battalion aid stations, field hospitals, gas hospitals, ambulance pools, the Collège de Juilly itself. Everywhere he went he found overworked doctors and sanitary men, inadequate facilities, and, especially, insufficient transportation. Shocked and angered, he fired off a scathing telegram to his editor, castigating the medical department of the Army for "failure to live up to its responsibilities." Why, he wanted to know, were there no evacuation hospitals closer to the front than Juilly during the first phase of the battle for Belleau Wood? Why were no field hospitals installed and functioning until June 9? Why were no attendants accompanying the wounded in the ambulances? Why were the dead left in the fields for days, allowed to bloat and turn black in the sun, and then dumped into shell holes or shallow graves and covered with a few spadefuls of earth? And why were more than ten per cent of these dead buried unidentified?

The censor refused to allow the telegram to go through: it was too hot. He forwarded it to A.E.F. headquarters, and Major General A.W. Brewster of the Inspector General's Office made an immediate investigation. The investigation bore out Whitney's charges: the medical situation was indeed disgraceful. But when the reasons for this were explained to the correspondent, he agreed to withdraw his telegram. It was apparent that the fault lay mostly with the French, who failed utterly to live up to their obligations, and that the medical department was doing everything possible to remedy the situation. And so none of these unsavory facts, which were responsible for the deaths of some men, the mutilation of others, and needless agony for many more, came out until long after the war was over.

CHAPTER 8

IF the newspaper accounts could be believed, the marines on June 6 had won the greatest victory since the Greeks defeated the Persians at Thermopylae. At last the reporters and military analysts had something they could get their teeth into, something more substantial than minor trench raids to crow about, and they made the most of it. On June 7 the headlines of the usually staid New York *Times* read: OUR TROOPS RESISTLESS. MOVING OUT TO "YANKEE DOODLE" THEY SWEEP ENEMY FROM THE HILLS . . . WHOLE DETACHMENTS OF GERMANS WIPED OUT . . . NO HOLDING BACK OUR MEN. Other newspapers were even more enthusiastic, especially the Chicago *Tribune,* which could boast of a "heroic" correspondent who had lost an eye in the battle. Belleau Wood became overnight a household name, evoking in the mind of the unsophisticated American public a romantic picture of grim-faced marines charging through trackless jungle with gleaming, blood-stained bayonets, leaving in their wake piles of dead and wounded Germans. The Marine Corps became the toast of the nation. Lines of eager young men appeared before recruiting offices throughout the country, and enlistments jumped over a hundred per cent in two days. Businessmen tried to cash in on the free publicity by running "clever" advertisements, one of which read: "As Our Marines Rout the Huns—So Monroe Clothes Rout High Prices." The reactions abroad were equally enthusiastic. Lloyd George lauded the marines for their "superb valor and skill," and Foch issued an official communiqué that praised the Americans and at the same time let the world know that the French too had taken part in the battle. "The courage of officers and men approached recklessness," the communiqué read in part. "Their help was just what we expected from gallant soldiers. They have won the admiration of the French troops with whom they fought."

Pershing was not pleased by the disproportionate amount of publicity received by the marines; it only added fuel to the rivalry that traditionally existed between the Army and the Marine Corps. Disgruntled division commanders complained to him about "eight thousand marines having won the war at Belleau Wood"; there was a marked increase in the number of brawls between marines and soldiers on leave in Paris; and within the 2nd Division itself, as we shall see, there was growing bad feeling between the marine and infantry regiments, and in particular between General Bundy and General Harbord. Pershing reprimanded the censor for allowing the correspondents to mention "marines" in their dispatches and ordered the practice to cease forthwith. He did not hesitate, however, to use the publicity to strengthen his own position vis-à-vis the Allied commanders. On the morning of June 7 he called on General Pétain in Compiègne and, holding the marines up as typical examples of the American fighting man, extracted permission to form an American corps front behind Château-Thierry, thus bringing an independent American Army one step nearer reality. (This diplomatic coup was highly gratifying to Pershing, but not, apparently, as gratifying as the compliment paid him at lunch the following day by Otto Kahn, the multimillionaire industrialist and financier who was visiting Paris on a semi-official mission for President Wilson. "As Commander-in-Chief of the A.E.F.," Kahn told Pershing—and the latter carefully noted it in his diary, "your duties embrace those of the Secretary of War, Secretary of the Treasury, and Secretary of State combined.")

Despite all the hullaballoo, however, neither the Chamber of Deputies nor the Supreme War Council unpacked their crates of records and relaxed. They were still prepared to move to Bordeaux at a moment's notice. They knew that the battle to save Paris was just beginning. And the population of the "City of Light," conditioned by years of lies and half-truths to minimize reports of victory, and still bedeviled by the three "Big Berthas," continued to leave the capital in droves.

DAWN on June 7 was overcast, chilly, threatening rain. Not a breath of air stirred in the swathes of mingled fog and smoke that collected in the hollows of Belleau Wood and the surrounding fields. It was perfect weather for a gas attack, and Harbord ordered the marines to keep their masks at the "alert" position at all times. Indeed, when Lieutenant Moore returned from his daring night ride into Bouresches with ammunition, he reported to brigade headquarters that the Germans were using a new gas on the road to Lucy-le-Bocage. It was heavy, he said, and tickled the nose and burned the throat. Also, he said, mistakenly, the mask was no protection against it. The Germans, however, were not yet ready to unleash a full-scale gas attack. That was still to come.

Lieutenant Colonel Lee, prodded no doubt by Harbord's irate message of the day before, personally inspected the front line and reported that "the situation looks better this morning. Holcomb occupies Bouresches with H Company. His line is organized and consolidated from Bouresches to Triangle Farm [about half a mile to the south]. He is in close touch with Sibley on his left and the 23rd Infantry on his right. H Company took Bouresches alone after a splendid fight with heavy losses.

F Company has about one effective platoon left. Holcomb reports that he has plenty of ammunition but needs rations. He requests that they be sent to Bouresches by truck."

Rations were short in both Bouresches and Belleau Wood, for the road from Lucy-le-Bocage was under enemy observation and men or vehicles moving along it were certain to be shelled and machine-gunned. Holcomb's men temporarily solved the problem by butchering a pig, a cow, and several chickens that they found wandering about the village—and this time there was no nonsense about "Allied" livestock being sacrosanct. The marines must have been hungry indeed, for they literally risked their lives to get these animals. The Germans had set up a machine gun in the railroad station, which was in a hollow just beyond the village, and sprayed anything that moved in the streets. Sibley's men found no livestock. They were forced to eat their remaining cans of cold "monkey meat" and to suck pebbles to assuage their thirst until runners could get through with full canteens. Some of them drank muddy water that seeped up into their foxholes—and got violent cramps. "This looks to me like a big emergency," Major Evans, the 6th's adjutant, reported to brigade headquarters. "If you can put it through to get a truck tonight, I am game to try to take it into Bouresches, and can find volunteers. It's worth a try for I am sick of thinking about it. I can also take water out of Sibley and drop it on the road and hustle it down the ravine."

Food and water remained a problem throughout the battle for Belleau Wood. Every night ration parties of thirty or more men set out from the rolling kitchens, four miles behind the lines, for the front. It was dirty, dangerous work—stumbling along rutted trails in pitch blackness with heavy "marmites" full of hot coffee and stew, tripping over roots, falling into shell holes, forced to drop everything and hit the ground when German artillery began landing among them, as it did at frequent intervals. Casualties were heavy: one of these ration parties, for example, reached Sibley with only six men left unwounded out of thirty-five who had started out. Before the battle was over, the paths leading to the woods and to

Bouresches were strewn with loaves of bread and spilled "slum."

June 7 was fairly quiet on the marines' front. Sibley's men, helped by two companies of engineers, reinforced their toe hold on the southern edge of the woods, rested when they had the chance, and waited for Stokes mortars and hand grenades to be brought up before renewing the assault. And Holcomb's troops had all they could do to hold Bouresches against unrelenting German pressure. But the French divisions on both flanks took advantage of the early morning fog to attack behind short, intense artillery barrages. The 167th on the left succeeded in driving the Germans back across the Clignon River; but the 10th Colonial on the right was stopped in its tracks by fresh troops of the German 28th Infantry Division, which had begun moving into the line during the night. The French captured several prisoners from the 28th and, under interrogation, they said that another division, the 5th Prussian Guards, was also coming into the line (to relieve the 197th Division, which held Bussiares and the northern lobe of Belleau Wood) and had orders to counterattack within a couple of days—"using lots of gas." This confirmed French intelligence reports from the Noyon-Montdidier sector, which said that pressure there had eased as German divisions were shunted south to face the 2nd Division.

Foch was pleased by this turn of events: it gave him a breathing spell during which he could move reinforcements down from Amiens. The news, however, was not nearly as reassuring to the officers of the 2nd Division, especially when it was supplemented by a telephone call from XXI Corps headquarters. "We have intercepted a German message," the caller, a French intelligence officer, said to Colonel Brown, "which directs that all the roads leading to Bouresches from the north, west, and south be placed under heavy artillery and machine-gun fire. This may indicate an attempt to isolate your garrison and an attack and attempt to capture it."

Shortly after this call was made, a runner arrived at division headquarters with background information on the German reinforcements. According to this information, the 5th Prussian Guards and the 28th Infantry were two of the best remaining divisions in the German Army. The Guards, under Major General von Haxthausen, were storm troopers, specialists in attack and counterattack, and had the distinction of being the first German troops to cross the Marne in 1914. They had received special training in open warfare and had played an important role in the attack on Amiens the previous March. The 28th Infantry was known as "The Conquerors of Lorette," had fought at Verdun in 1917, at Cambrai in the German counteroffensive of the same year, and on the Somme in the spring of 1918.

The Germans were indeed paying special attention to the 2nd Division; the 28th Infantry's daily report for June 8 was specific on this point. "The 2nd Division," the report read, "which made the attack on June 6 . . . is probably no longer very efficient. There are no signs that the enemy has serious attack intentions on the corps front. The enemy intends to gain the following things: immobilization of the German forces and local improvement of his line. It will also give the Americans an opportunity for cheap successes. These are then to be headlined in the newspapers. It will be said that *one* American division has been sufficient to stop German attacks without difficulty. Further inferences will be left to the public—and they will probably run like this: 'As soon as the already frequently heralded American divisions have arrived, then the war will be easily won from the central powers.' Should the Americans on our front gain the upper hand even temporarily, this may have the most unfavorable influence on the morale of the central powers and on continuation of the war. In the fighting that faces us, therefore, it is not a matter of possession or non-possession of a village or wood, of indifferent value of itself, but a question of whether English-American publicity will succeed in representing the American Army as one equal to the German Army or as actually superior troops. The renewed employment of the 5th Guard and the 28th Infantry Divisions in the front line of the Corps Conta is to be considered from this point of view."

Both the Americans and the Germans, then, placed more importance on the battle than the amount of terrain concerned would seem to warrant. Prestige, "psychological mastery," were involved: it was a small pivot upon which great events could turn. . . .

During the night Major Evans succeeded in reaching Sibley with several Stokes mortars and an adequate supply of hand grenades, and at 4:00 A.M. on June 8 the marines tried once more to advance into the woods. In the meantime, several hours earlier, the Germans had launched a determined attack against Bouresches and the 23rd Infantry positions south of it.

Neither side made much progress. Harbord had reinforced the garrison in Bouresches with two companies of the 4th Machine Gun Battalion under Major Edmund Zane, and with two companies of engineers. One machine-gun platoon set up its guns on the side of the village facing the railroad embankment, barely two hundred yards distant. (The company commander, Captain Andrew Bruce, requested that automatic rifles be substituted for machine guns in this platoon. "The range is so short," he said, "that machine guns are wasted and easily captured." But his request was denied.) The other platoons emplaced their guns on the slope behind the village where they commanded all approaches to the valley with plunging fire. "It's going to be hell on the wounded," Bruce's report continued. "Practically impossible to get anyone out in daylight from the dressing station, because that draw leading in is under direct observation and artillery fire. It's bad enough for the ration details at night. They simply dodge shells along that ravine for over half a mile."

The marines suffered few casualties in this attack, however, for the Germans were quickly pinned down by the machine guns and forced to retreat behind the railroad embankment. One of Lieutenant Robertson's men, Corporal H. A. Leonard, captured a wounded *feldwebel* during the fight and dragged him back to the company's post of command, which was in the cellar of a farmhouse. Under interrogation he said that his company had been ordered to hold the embankment "at all costs." The *feldwebel* was from Berlin and had lived in the States for several years before the war. "When this is over," he told Leonard, "I'm going to get the family and move back to

Philadelphia." Leonard was outraged: just a few minutes ago this man had been trying to kill him. "Get that idea out of your head!" he snapped. "We'll have lynching parties waiting for all you Heinies!"

Sibley's attack started promisingly enough—though his men were near exhaustion, unshaven, filthy, and had not had a hot meal or changed their clothes in ten days. Sergeant Robert Donaghue won a Distinguished Service Cross by capturing a Maxim and killing its crew before he himself was evacuated with a severe wound, and another gun was knocked out of action by hand grenades. But Major Bischoff's Maxims were too much for Sibley. He continued trying until shortly after 10:00 A.M., when he reported to brigade headquarters: "They are too strong for us. As soon as we take one machine gun another opens up on us. The losses are so heavy that I am re-forming on ground held last night by I Company. All officers of I Company wounded or missing. Necessary to reform before we can advance. Unable to use trench mortars because of woods. These machine guns are too strong for our infantry. We can attack again if it is desired."

It was not desired. Sibley's reports made it clear that his men had absorbed all the punishment they could stand—despite his gallant offer at the end of the above message—and with the woods so strongly held Harbord realized that other tactics were called for. He spent the morning of June 8 in conference with Brigadier General William Chamberlaine, commander of the division's artillery brigade, and arranged with him for a combined artillery and infantry attack on the morning of June 10. Harbord's plan was this: the artillery—thirty batteries of 75's and twelve of 155's (including nine light batteries borrowed from the French)—would blast the woods throughout the night, and towards dawn lay down a rolling barrage behind which Major John A. Hughes's battalion of the 6th Marines, which had been held in reserve until then, would "sweep" the woods from south to north. Sibley was ordered to withdraw to the cover of "Gob Gully" and stay there until the bombardment was over and the attack well under way; then the survivors of his battalion would go into reserve near Lucy-le-Bocage.

ALL day on June 9 the "hairy cannoneers" trundled their guns into position, stacked up mounds of ammunition nearby, and with the help of airplane spotters, zeroed in on their respective targets. Starting just after dusk, they dropped a total of thirty-four thousand high-explosive shells into the woods and on the German positions behind Torcy and Bussiares, creating a continuous crackle and roar of blue flame, which seemed to Colonel Wise, who was still holding the ridge northwest of Belleau Wood, "as though someone were playing a giant searchlight up and down in the dark." (One of the 155's was badly aimed and caused forty casualties in the 23rd Infantry before its fire was corrected.) At 4:30 A.M., given close support by the 6th Machine Gun Battalion under Major Edward Cole, Hughes's troops entered the woods in four waves and began their sweep north. At first they met only light resistance, and Hughes reported to brigade headquarters that the artillery had "blown the Bois de Belleau to mincemeat."

This report, however, soon turned out to be premature. The woods had indeed been all but leveled in some parts, but the machine-gun nests within them were still very much intact—as Hughes learned to his cost. When the bombardment had started the night before, Major Bischoff had wisely abandoned his southernmost line of resistance—the weakest of the three—and had withdrawn his guns to the central and northern lines, which were well dug in and protected. Most of the artillery shells had contact fuses and exploded when they hit the tops of the trees. The trenches and dugouts beneath them were showered with shrapnel and broken branches, but there were relatively few casualties. And as soon as the barrage had passed beyond their positions, the Germans popped up behind their guns once more.

Major Cole, farther forward than he had any business being, was severely wounded in the hand, eye, and both legs. He died in the hospital a few days later. Captain Fuller was killed; Captain Burns had both legs blown off below the knees, a mortal wound; Lieutenant Dennis was all but cut in half by machine-gun bullets. Other officers and men began to go down, and the bulk of the marines, confused by the enemy's unexpectedly savage stand and

100

hampered by inadequate and out-of-date maps, took the line of least resistance and veered off towards the eastern boundary of the woods. The impetus of the attack swiftly died and by eight o'clock that morning all forward movement had ceased. But Major Hughes, as badly confused as his company commanders, and misinformed by their reports, sent a message to Harbord saying that all the objectives had been attained and consolidated. He was wrong: the objectives had not been attained. His men, in fact, were a good four hundred yards short of Bischoff's main line of defense across the narrow central part of the woods, and the northern lobe had hardly been touched at all.

It was not until later in the morning, however, when other reports began to come in, that Harbord became aware of the true situation. He was embarrassed and annoyed, for he had reported to both division and corps headquarters that the woods had been completely cleaned out. He immediately sent a motorcycle with sidecar to pick up Colonel Wise and bring him to La Loge.

"Wise," he said when the colonel arrived, "the Sixth have made two attacks on Belleau Wood. The first one failed; the second made a little headway on the southern edge. You're on the ground there. You know the conditions. It's up to you to clean it up. Go ahead and make your own plans and do the job."

"Very well, sir."

"Do you want artillery assistance?"

"No, sir. With the small amount we have, it only warns the Germans that the attack is coming."

Wise thought he saw a way to accomplish his mission with a minimum of casualties. He determined to attack the Germans from the rear, between the railroad embankment that followed the course of the Clignon River, and the northern edge of the woods. This plan had one major drawback: it would expose his men to fire from the enemy support units behind the embankment. But the chances of success, he estimated, were worth running this risk. On the way back to the ridge to rejoin his troops, he stopped at 5th Regiment headquarters in La Voie du Chatel and asked Colonel Neville to restore his battalion to full strength by returning Captain Lloyd Williams' company, which had been detached several days earlier for service with Major Turrill. Then he sent for his company commanders, filled them in on the situation, and set the zero hour for four o'clock. Every man in the battalion, he said, was to carry two extra bandoliers of ammunition in addition to the regulation one hundred rounds.

It began to rain during the night, an intermittent drizzle that chilled the men to the bone and kept them huddling, sleepless, beneath their ponchos. At midnight a runner came up to Wise's post of command and handed him a message from brigade headquarters. Wise took it under his poncho and flicked on his flashlight to read it. He turned pale and blinked his eyes in disbelief. Harbord had changed his mind, had withdrawn Wise's carte blanche. The colonel was now ordered to attack from the south behind a rolling barrage, join his right flank to Hughes's left, and push through the woods. "I felt sick," he wrote later. "I knew that that piece of paper meant needless death for most of my battalion. A frontal attack against a prepared position." But he had no choice. He called in his company commanders again and gave them the new orders. "The front assigned for the attack is so wide," he told them, "that I'm going to risk putting all four companies in the line. There'll be no supports or reserves, so it's no good sending back for reinforcements."

At 3:00 A.M. the weary troops slogged south past Lucy-le-Bocage and spread out in a line of skirmishers across the fields facing the southern edge of the woods. A few birds called and an airplane hummed in the distance. Otherwise there was silence. Wise established his post of command in a clump of trees about half a mile from the woods, gathered a group of runners about him, and waited for the barrage to signal the attack.

At three-forty-five the artillery opened fire on the woods and, in between explosions, Wise could hear the German machine guns coming to life, firing short tentative bursts, as though clearing their throats. All chances of taking the enemy by surprise were now gone. Then the company commanders blew their whistles and the men rose with fixed bayonets and started forward. Lieutenant S. C. Cummings, a platoon leader, described the early part of the advance in a letter. ". . . The arm motion forward was given," he wrote, "and line after line moved toward the woods six hundred yards away across an open and level field covered with grass about six inches high. The ground became covered with a sheet of machine-gun fire. We moved forward at a slow pace, keeping perfect lines. Men were being mowed down like wheat. A whiz-bang hit on my right and an automatic rifle team disappeared, while men on left and right were armless, legless, or tearing at their faces. We continued to advance until about fifty yards from the woods, when something hit me and I spun around and hit flat. I didn't know where I was hit, so I jumped up to go forward again, but fell. I crawled to a shellhole nearby. I don't see how I ever got there as the ground was being plowed by machine guns. . . . It happened to be one made by a trench mortar and was about six feet deep and ten feet across. I put on a dressing and started figuring on how to get back to the first-aid station. Shells were still lighting around, shrapnel bursting, machine gun bullets passing overhead—and they mingled with the screams and cries of the wounded and dying. On cleaning out the woods a sniper, undoubtedly up a tree, had been left behind. From the sound of his rifle I figured he was about fifty yards away and was picking off any wounded who were moving and had not reached cover. I had lost the rifle that I was carrying, so I decided to try my Colt .45 on him. I crawled to the edge of the shellhole and heard a ping. Deciding that discretion was the better part of valor, I got down in the shellhole again and looked at my pistol to find it minus a front sight. I got picked up by stretcher bearers and went through battalion and regimental dressing stations and then in an ambulance to the evacuation hospital."

Private F. E. Steck of Captain Williams' company also described the action. "We came across a German officer seated comfortably with his knees crossed," Steck wrote. "Before him was spread a little field table on which was cake, jam, cookies, and a fine array of food. A knife and fork was in either hand. Beside the officer was seated a large, bulky sergeant who had been knitting socks. The darning needles were still between his fingers. Both their heads had been blown off by a large shell. . . . My duties were to load a Chauchat . . . You could run about nine steps and then another clip would have to be inserted. Bullets slit my canteen, hit my scabbard, and two or three went through my trousers without touching me. We had advanced in triangle formation about half a mile. I was in the front end of the 'V' when three machine gun bullets got me. One went into my neck, another in my left shoulder, and the third in my arm. I tried to keep on in assisting the operation of the automatic but the blood came up in my throat. I forced my way back and hid in a shellhole in the woods until a little marine found me. This fellow dragged me five hundred yards on his shoulder to a first-aid dugout. There a shelter-half was used as a stretcher and I was taken back to a larger dressing station."

Actually, despite the heavy losses, the attack was going better than Wise had any reason to expect. The barrage and the previous attacks had weakened the enemy and, despite their extreme fatigue, the marines' morale was still excellent. Not so the Germans'. A letter taken from the body of a Private Hebel of the 237th Infantry Division substantiates this. "We are having very heavy days with death before us hourly," Hebel had written. "Here we have no hope of coming out. My company has been reduced from a hundred and twenty to thirty men. Oh, what misery! We are now at the worst stage of the offensive, the time of counter-attacks. We have Americans opposite us who are terribly reckless fellows. In the last eight days I have not slept twenty hours."

The hardest fighting took place along the eastern edge of the woods, which was defended by the 40th Fusilier Regiment of the 28th Division. This regiment lost over seven hundred killed, wounded, and captured, and in a report following the action, said that the Americans attacked in "gangs of ten to twenty men, primed with alcohol. Some of their wounded kept on in the attack. Our men threw hand grenades into these gangs but were simply ignored by the enemy. They had no idea of tactical principles. They fired while walking with their rifles under their arms. They carried light machine guns with them—no hand grenades, but knives, revolvers, rifle butts and bayonets. All were big fellows, powerful, rowdies. They had no sort of leadership. . . . Even with the forces now employed," the report pessimistically concluded, "it will hardly be possible to hold Belleau Wood in the event of a renewed hostile attack, which can be expected tomorrow or the day after."

Wise's men had trouble finding Hughes's in the confusion of battle, and the plan for a combined sweep of the woods had to be abandoned. "Nothing in our training had foreseen fighting like this," Wise commented. "If there was any strategy, it was the strategy of the red Indian." Wise's battalion lost over two hundred and fifty men, including Captain Williams (who had said "Retreat, hell! We just got here!"), but the marines captured many machine guns, several trench mortars, and over a hundred and fifty prisoners, including three officers. Most of the captured Maxims had wheelbarrows or baby carriages full of ammunition beside them, so the marines were able to turn the guns against the enemy. (Major Bischoff noticed this and ordered his men henceforth to remove the bolts from the Maxims if they were obliged to retreat.) The prisoners were convoyed by wounded marines to Wise's post of command, briefly questioned, then their shoelaces were cut and they were sent back to brigade headquarters. Except for one or two die-hard patriots among them who maintained tight-lipped silence and only glared at their captors with contempt, they all said they were fed up with the war and glad to be out of it.

The Germans, however, reacted violently to the attack, throwing in a battalion of the 36th Infantry Division to reinforce Major Bischoff at a crucial moment, and placing Lucy-le-Bocage and all the main roads under "neutralization" fire by artillery. The 150's and 210's rained down at the rate of ten per minute, blew up two ammunition dumps, utterly destroyed the village, and caused seventy casualties, most of them German prisoners. One of the shells burst in a battalion dressing station, setting it on fire, and three pharmacist's mates won Distinguished Service Crosses by carrying out the wounded and medical instruments and bandages.

According to the reports Wise had received from his company commanders, the woods had been cleaned out and all the objectives attained. But early in the afternoon, when he made a personal inspection of the positions, he discovered that most of the northern lobe was still in the enemy's hands. In the meantime he had reported to Harbord that "Belleau Wood belongs to the 5th Marines" and the general had repeated the message to division and corps headquarters, embarrassing himself for the second time in two days.

For the moment, at least, there was nothing to be done about it. The marines were exhausted after their morning's fight, and Harbord realized that there was no possibility of mounting another attack until the positions had been thoroughly consolidated and replacements received.

CHAPTER 9

THE replacements—"overshirts" was their code name —looked rather dazed and bewildered as they filed up the dusty road towards La Voie du Chatel on the afternoon of June 11. Their forest-green uniforms still had the sheen of newness (the veterans of the 5th and 6th Regiments had long since worn theirs out and were dressed in Army khaki), and they sweltered beneath the weight of their heavy packs and weapons. Behind them were the busy weeks in Quantico and Parris Island, the voyage to Brest in the overcrowded transport, and a short period of training around St. Aignan ("Saint Onion")—"where the women and the omelets were first-rate and the white wine tasted lots better than the chlorinated water." Now, under the tender guidance of a red-necked sergeant with a double row of ribbons on his tunic and a string of hashmarks running up his sleeve, they were headed towards their baptism of fire.

All around them were the signs of war: the blackened ruins of farmhouses and barns, some of them still smoldering and giving off that unmistakable acrid odor of things burning that ought not to be burning; here and there in the fields were dead cows, horses, and mules, their legs jutting up out of their bloated bodies like pins out of a pincushion, filling the air with a noxious stench that made the men cough and exclaim in disgust. Far ahead, floating like fat gray sausages above the woods and fields, they could see German observation balloons, and, farther still, a dark moving speck surrounded by white puffballs that was an enemy airplane, and bursting antiaircraft shells. In the distance there was a faint drumming of artillery and the sporadic crackling of machine guns and automatic rifles.

At 5th Regiment headquarters they were split up into consignments for the various battalions—150 to Colonel Wise, 170 to Major Turrill, 200 to Major Shearer (a similar division was taking place at the 6th Marines' post of command); then the sergeant bawled at them, "All right, you boots—fall out alongside the road and make combat packs. We'll stay here till dark."

"At ten o'clock that night," a replacement for Major Turrill's battalion wrote, "we were given two boxes of hardtack and a double handful of dried prunes apiece; then we formed up on both sides of the road, five yards between each man, and started out. There was no smoking and no talking. It was dark and cloudy and we stumbled along in the blackness cursing when we bumped into the man ahead. We went along the road for a couple of miles, through a deserted village, and then, passing through a hedge, we entered a wood-cutter's path through a forest. A few minutes later Heinie artillery started coming in. There was a flash and a roar from somewhere up ahead and I heard a man cry out. We hit the ground and waited for the bombardment to end; all around us there was the crackling of breaking trees and the patter of shrapnel on the ground. Then we went on. I passed a wrecked ammunition cart and a smoking hole in the middle of the path with a dead mule lying beside it. There was a little group of marines in the brush alongside the path. A wounded man was groaning 'Oh, Jesus! Jesus Christ! Oh, Jesus!' and I caught a glimpse of bloodstained bandages. My knees felt suddenly weak and I wanted to sit down. 'Move along there,' the sergeant growled, 'unless you want your Ma to stick a red star in

her window.' . . . I guessed we were in Belleau Wood."
(He was wrong; he was in Champillon Wood about a
mile to the west.)

ON the morning of June 12 General Harbord held a conference in brigade headquarters with his regimental and
battalion commanders. Reports from reconnaissance patrols that had probed the German lines during the night
gave the impression that, while the enemy still held the
northern lobe of the woods, their position was precarious
and a determined thrust could drive them out. This was
Colonel Wise's opinion also. "It didn't look like a very
hard nut to crack," he wrote. "Slightly higher ground.
Same tall trees, same underbrush, same boulders." He
thought his men could take it, he told Harbord, provided
they had some artillery support.

Harbord was annoyed with Wise. Thanks to the colonel's false report that the woods had been cleaned out,
the Brigade Commander had been made to look foolish
in the eyes of General Bundy and General Degoutte. By
rights Major Turrill's battalion, which was somewhat
rested, should have made this new attack. But, perhaps to
give Wise a chance to amend his blunder, Harbord told
him to go ahead and make the assault on the northern
lobe at 5:00 P.M. The overall plan, he said, would be the
same as for the attack on June 11: Wise's men would join
forces with Hughes's, who were still holding the southern and eastern edges of the wood, and sweep north.

When he returned to his post of command later that
afternoon, Wise telephoned brigade headquarters and
asked for an additional half-hour's artillery preparation,
so the attack did not start until five-thirty. Once again it
was savage "red Indian"-style warfare with groups of men
firing from the hip, moving from tree to tree, and charging with fixed bayonets. Captain Dunbeck, one of Wise's
two remaining company commanders, was wounded and
his place was taken by Lieutenant Drinkard Milner, a
soft-spoken minister's son. At eight-thirty that night, after
three hours of continuous fighting, Wise's men emerged
on the northern edge of the woods. At last—or so it
seemed—Belleau Wood was "Marine Corps' property entire." In the two-day battle the marines had captured sixty

machine guns, ten trench mortars, and over four hundred prisoners. But their own losses had been staggering. Wise had three hundred men left in his battalion—a casualty rate of seventy per cent—and only one officer per company. Hughes was in slightly better shape with seven hundred survivors. The losses, in fact, were so severe that, despite the replacements who had arrived the day before, Wise asked brigade headquarters to supply ration-carrying details. "All of mine are fighting," he told Harbord. "So far it has been very hard to get runners through. Some have never returned. Morale excellent, but everybody about all in."

Among the prisoners taken on the afternoon of June 12 were a wounded officer and forty-two men who, surrounded in a thicket, surrendered under a white flag. The officer informed Colonel Wise that the German IV Reserve Corps planned a counterattack under the code name *Uberseefahrt* (Overseas Voyage) for the following morning. The attack would be made along the entire front, including Belleau Wood, Bouresches, and the 3rd Brigade's positions south of it, and would be preceded by a massive artillery barrage. Wise passed this information along to brigade headquarters and was ordered to close his line to the right and join forces with Major Hughes's battalion. He objected that this would force him to abandon his hard-won territory in the northwest corner of the woods, but was told that he had no choice: there were not enough marines left to defend the entire wood. Indeed, the situation was so critical that Colonel Brown took the unusual step of sending a special emissary to look over the marines' positions in the woods. "Impress upon them not only the necessity of echeloning in depth," the colonel told his emissary, Major Brabson, "but also being able to hold the old line they had near Lucy-le-Bocage. They should wire in at once. The engineers should be called upon to get the material. There is not a moment to lose wiring in these positions. The 24th Division is reported relieving the 197th Division for the purpose of attack. *Wire!*"

As Wise's men vacated the northwest corner of the woods, too weary even to wonder about this apparently senseless move, German troops of the 237th Division filtered back in with machine guns and mortars. They applied immediate pressure to Wise's left flank, and by nightfall the colonel was forced to bend his line back to face north—to "refuse his flank," in military parlance. This position soon became infamous as "The Hook."

ON the day before, June 11, General Harbord had sent a long report to General Bundy covering the events of the preceding three days and concluding with the following paragraph:

"I desire to call attention of the division commander to the fact that this brigade has been in the line since June 1 to date and has been almost continuously fighting. Its line has receded nowhere, and has everywhere advanced. Officers and men are now at a state scarcely less than complete physical exhaustion. Men fall asleep under bombardment, and the physical exhaustion and the heavy losses are a combination calculated to damage morale, which should be met by immediate arrangements for the relief of this brigade. The talk among officers and soldiers of the French Army, whom this brigade relieved, appeared to be that constant fighting for five or six days by them excused them for falling back before the enemy. This brigade has more than doubled the time which they [the French] considered exhausted them and has advanced against and held the enemy during all that time. I cannot too strongly urge that immediate arrangements be made for its relief, to enable us to rest and reorganize."

When he got this message, Bundy sent a telegram to A.E.F. headquarters requesting that the marine brigade be relieved. He was told that no relief was available. Nevertheless the wheels began to turn, telegrams and messages flew back and forth among the various French and American headquarters, and several investigations were made of the situation. One of these investigations was carried out by Major Richardson on behalf of Colonel Fox Conner, Pershing's adjutant. Here is the text of their telephone conversation on the afternoon of June 12:

Major Richardson: The situation is as reported. General Lewis' brigade could stay. General Harbord's could not. I do not recommend relief by brigade of the 4th

Division [this had been discussed earlier]. They lack machine guns, machine rifles, rifles, and transportation, and they have no signal battalion. One of its regiments has had almost no target practice. In taking it over I think it would be better to relieve the entire division for a couple of weeks. That would be the better solution. I do think that General Harbord's brigade should be relieved.

Colonel Conner: Did you talk to General Harbord?

Major Richardson: Yes sir, I did. He was very emphatic that if they have another attack, which they think they will have, he does not believe they would stand it. After talking with General Bundy, Colonel Brown, and General Lewis, I think General Lewis' brigade could stand: I do not think General Harbord's brigade could.

Colonel Conner: When do you think they should be relieved?

Major Richardson: I think it should be just as soon as possible.

THE propaganda war, meanwhile, went on apace, with each side claiming resounding victories. The New York *Times* headline on June 12 read: OUR MEN TAKE BELLEAU WOOD. THREE HUNDRED CAPTIVES. Several of the inside pages were devoted to an analysis, generally false, of the strategical importance of Belleau Wood, and others to first-person accounts of the battle, equally unreliable and full of hyperbole. The German High Command, through its semiofficial Wolff Bureau in Amsterdam, said: "For the first time an American division advanced to the attack on the front northwest of Château-Thierry. The hottest point was Belleau Wood, where a German regiment inflicted severe losses and repulsed the Americans who got as far as the edge of the wood in a fight at close quarters with hand grenades and bayonets. Nevertheless, parts of the American division, notably a naval brigade, advanced again to the attack in successive waves. We allowed the enemy to approach closely. Near the edge of the wood they were caught in front and on both flanks by a withering machine gun and artillery fire. Only a few of the Americans escaped by surrender or by hasty flight to the rear. Heaps of Ameri-

111

can dead lie on the front of Belleau Wood." And Ludendorff supplemented this statement with another, which said: "Stubbornly, and shunning no sacrifices, the enemy continued his ill-fated attack northwest of Château-Thierry. Repeated assaults here collapsed with bloody losses."

It remained to be seen, however, if the attack was truly "ill-fated."

THE anticipated German counterattack came at four o'clock on the morning of June 13. Throughout the night the enemy artillery pounded the woods, Bouresches, and the 23rd and 9th Infantry positions with 150's and 210's, including shells that contained sneezing and vomiting gas. (The gas inadvertently saved Colonel Wise's life, for it forced him to vacate a ditch near his post of command just a few seconds before a high-explosive shell scored a direct hit on it.) Some of the 210's that were dropped on Bouresches had twenty-second delayed-action fuses so that they would bury themselves deep within the foundations of a house before going off. The intensity of the bombardment was between "harassing" and "neutralization" and caused "fairly heavy casualties" (twenty per cent in Major Hughes's battalion alone). It also had a terribly demoralizing effect on the men who escaped unscathed—leaving them deafened, shaken, and sleepless to face the attacking infantry at dawn.

The attack on Bouresches was the most severe. It was undertaken by the 109th Grenadiers and the 40th Fusiliers, both of the 28th Division. The Grenadiers attacked from the south, captured several farmhouses and the ruins of the church, and forced the marines to retire behind street barricades in the center of the village. From this point, however, the Americans refused to be dislodged, but fought back fiercely with machine guns and rifle grenades. The German commander was wounded, but his men held on to the ground they had captured. They were waiting for the 40th Fusiliers' attack to develop from the east and north. This, however, never took place, for the Fusiliers were pinned down by machine guns and artillery and were forced to retire behind the embankment once more. At 9:30 A.M. the attack was called off and the commanding general of Corps Conta heaped bitter recriminations on "The Conquerors of Lorette" for their failure to advance. The Grenadiers in Bouresches held on for another hour or so, then abandoned their advanced position and retreated to the jump-off line. *Uberseefahrt* had been a short voyage indeed.

In the meantime Major Elliott of the 23rd, apprised of the dangerous situation in the village, had sent in reinforcements. One group was under a lieutenant named Villmuth, who was wounded as he approached Bouresches and sent back a panicky message saying that the Germans had captured the village and that the artillery should open fire on it immediately. Major Hughes, in the woods, also reported that the German attack was making headway, but Harbord, forwarding the message to division headquarters, added: "Major Hughes has been under a tremendous strain for a long time and I don't feel like crediting that information as very reliable." Neither did Harbord allow himself to be stampeded by Lieutenant Villmuth's message, but refused to order artillery fire on Bouresches until the lieutenant's report had been confirmed. This was just as well, for Major Shearer (Major Berry's successor) informed him an hour later that the marines had repulsed the attack and still held the village.

In the woods, the Germans reinforced their hold on the northwest corner but could not make a dent in the marines' lines, though the fighting swirled viciously around "The Hook" and the casualties were heavy. Colonel Wise had another narrow escape. He was seated on the edge of a ditch, giving instructions to two machine-gun officers, when a "whiz-bang" exploded above his head. The officer on his right was killed and the one on his left wounded. A shell fragment ripped through the colonel's blouse but did not touch him.

When he returned to his post of command a little later in the day, Wise found the Reverend Doctor Larned, a chaplain, waiting for him. Doctor Larned, a bespectacled man of about forty, was the former rector of an exclusive Episcopalian church in Bar Harbor, Maine, and had come directly from there to France. "What shall I do?" he asked Wise.

"If you want to live," the colonel told him, "you'd better get an entrenching tool and start digging."

That was sound advice for anyone in or near Belleau Wood, for the German counterattacks were far from over.

CHAPTER 10

"GAS!"

This cry of alarm, accompanied by the raucous hooting of an air horn or the clang of metal on metal as the gas guard beat a frenzied tocsin on an empty shell-casing with a hammer, was probably the most frightening sound that a soldier in the First World War could hear. Panic and hysteria almost invariably followed—men fumbling open the stiff canvas bag hanging at their sides, clapping the mask on their faces, clutching their rifles with sweaty hands, and peering apprehensively through striated yellowish eyepieces at a world gone suddenly as dim and vague as an old print of a film.

Merely to wear the mask was excruciatingly uncomfortable. "If anyone wants to know how a gas mask feels," wrote Major Boyce of the 3rd Division, "let him seize his nose with a pair of fire tongs, bury his face in a hot feather pillow, then seize a gas pipe with his teeth and breathe through it for a few hours while he performs routine duties. It is safe but, like the deadly poison which forced its invention, it is not sane." Yet men were often required not only to perform routine duties while wearing their masks, but to fight with them on as well.

As a killer of men, poison gas was in no way comparable to artillery and machine guns; for every soldier who died in a gas attack, hundreds were slaughtered by shells and bullets. But shells and bullets possess one distinct virtue: they manifest themselves in concrete

114

ways—roaring overhead like express trains through a tunnel, crackling, buzzing, digging up the earth, even smashing through flesh and bone. They can be heard and felt and sometimes seen: they lend a focus to fear. Gas, however, is an invisible killer, at once everywhere and nowhere, and men have always been most afraid of the unseen enemy.

Poison gas was introduced into the war by the Germans on April 22, 1915, when they launched the first "cloud attack" of chlorine against the French and Canadian troops at Ypres. The attack caused some fifteen thousand casualties, including five thousand dead, and would undoubtedly have caused more but for a knowledgeable Canadian in the trenches who told everyone within earshot to urinate on their handkerchiefs and hold them against their faces. The Germans had been somewhat dubious of the new weapon's effectiveness, despite the inventor's claims, and had not made any preparations to follow up the cloud attack with an infantry advance. Had they done so, they would certainly have overrun the Allied lines, for the French and Canadians were utterly demoralized and could have offered little resistance. Nevertheless the German High Command was well satisfied with the results of the experiment, and between 1915 and 1918 they developed and put into use a full-fledged armory of poison gases. They also developed a variety of methods of delivering these gases on the enemy and were no longer constrained by an adverse wind, as in a cloud attack.

The gases employed by both sides in the war fall into three general categories: irritants, suffocants, and vesicants. They were usually referred to, respectively, as "blue cross," "green cross," and "yellow cross," because of the identifying marks on the shells that contained them. The most common of the irritating gases (blue cross) was diphenylarsine. It was odorless and caused a burning sensation in the nose and throat, which was accompanied by sneezing, spitting, and sometimes vomiting. Of itself it was not especially serious, although a massive dose could incapacitate a man for several days; but it was serious indeed when used in conjunction with one of the suffocants, for it often forced a soldier to remove his mask in order to avoid strangling on his own vomit, and allowed the deadlier gas to enter his lungs. After a while the Germans developed a regular and highly effective method of employing this gas. When green troops entered the trenches opposite them, they would drop only diphenylarsine for a period of two or three weeks, lulling them into a false sense of security; then, when the psychological conditions were right, they would combine it with huge quantities of phosgene or chloropicrin, the most common of the suffocants (green cross), and cause heavy casualties.

The physiological effects of phosgene and chloropicrin were especially horrifying. Men who breathed in appreciable quantities of these gases died excruciatingly. Their lungs became heavy with fluid and swelled so that they completely filled the thoracic cavity and pressed up into the throat; their skins turned blue or, in some cases, ashy gray; and their blood acquired the color and consistency of melted chocolate. After a few hours or days of unspeakable agony, during which they gasped wildly and with diminishing success for breath, they died of suffocation.

The vesicants, mustard gas and lewisite, were the last to be developed, and the most effective. They were not quite as deadly as phosgene and chloropicrin, but they were easier to deliver on the enemy and they caused far more casualties. Mustard gas, also called yperite because it was first used at Ypres, is an oily liquid compound of carbon, hydrogen, chlorine, and sulphur, which readily vaporizes. The liquid, sprayed from a bursting shell, forms an invisible vapor that attacks the mucous membranes of the respiratory tract, destroys lung tissue when inhaled in minute quantities, blisters the skin, and causes severe conjunctivitis. It penetrates clothing, clings to the hair (men with long hair suffered most from it—hence the "G.I." haircut of World War II), seeks out the tenderest parts of the body to blister and burn—the scrotum, penis, the skin around the rectum, and inside the elbows, knees, and thighs. It remains for long periods on brush and trees, in water, on the earth itself, and was known to cause casualties, even death, as long as three weeks after it had been dropped on a given area. Because of its slow rate of dissipation, it was essentially a defensive weapon, and the Germans commonly used it to interdict certain areas to the enemy.

The Allies, of course, retaliated in kind, and a furious race began to see which side could produce the deadliest gases first, the most effective means of delivering them on the enemy, and the best defenses against them. The British performed most of their experiments at Hanlon Field, which was named after Corporal Peter Hanlon, the first casualty in the Royal Chemical Corps. They developed lewisite, similar in composition to mustard gas and equally effective; the Small Box Respirator (S.B.R.), which was used by United States troops until American scientists came up with one as good; and the Livens projector, a series of mortar tubes, fired by electrical contact, which could deliver from two hundred to eight hundred gas bombs simultaneously on the enemy lines. The Germans had a similar projector, with a range of fifteen hundred yards, and used it to saturate limited targets. Surprise was an essential factor in a gas attack, and, to avoid being spotted by enemy aircraft, these projectors had to be installed with great speed and secrecy, usually in the course of one night. Even so, the flash caused by hundreds of tubes being fired at once often warned the enemy troops and gave them time to put on their masks. The Germans also developed gas hand grenades, which proved impractical, and the high-explosive artillery shell containing ten per cent of phosgene or mustard, which allowed them to harass rear-echelon troops.

The French, with characteristic subtlety, concentrated on the development of camouflage gases. They discovered, for example, that butyl sulfide added to mustard gas gave it a skunk-like odor. When used in wooded areas in which skunks were common, this proved highly effective. They also developed a type of mustard gas that was more virulent and longer-lasting than the German equivalent.

The United States was the last country to enter this race, but by the end of 1918 it was producing more than twice as much poison gas as the other Allies and the Central Powers combined. Nor did the nation lag behind in the production of what might be called "gas ac-

117

cessories." By November, 1918, the Chemical Warfare Department shipped overseas four million gas masks, as well as huge quantities of bleaching powder (an oxydizer of mustard gas), antidimming fluid to prevent moisture from condensing on the eyepieces, sag paste (a protective ointment), dugout blanket oil, which helped stop gas from seeping into these shelters, and trench fans to clear the gassed areas.

Medical treatment of gas cases was a difficult problem, and special field hospitals were set up within a couple of thousand yards of the front lines. Rapid treatment was essential: an hour saved at the front could mean a week's less time in the hospital for the casualty. In the battalion dressing stations the wounded men's throats were sprayed with a solution of bicarbonate of soda, and gauze compresses soaked in the solution were placed on their eyes; sometimes, too, they were given injections of camphorated oil or caffein-citrate. Then, in the hospital, their clothing was removed and they were given hot showers or sponge baths to wash off the residue of the gas, were wrapped in blankets, and put to bed. For those with damaged lungs, there were tanks of pure oxygen to help them breathe. But that was all the doctors could do. There was no "cure" for gas poisoning, only amelioration and partial prevention. The troops were warned not to defecate or urinate in gassed areas, not to use the water for any purpose, not to lie on the ground or touch leaves or brush, not to burn logs in their dugouts, because the heat rapidly vaporized the mustard gas with which the wood was sometimes impregnated. But no cure was developed either during the war or afterward. Indeed, many thousands of men who were only "lightly touched" by poison gas suffered for the rest of their lives from weakened lungs and succumbed easily to grippe, pneumonia, bronchitis, tuberculosis, and other pulmonary ailments.

Gas discipline throughout the A.E.F., and especially in the 2nd Division, was notoriously poor. The youthful arrogance and high spirits of the troops (particularly the marines), which made them first-class fighting men in other respects, worked against them here. They seemed to feel there was something shameful about being afraid of gas, and, until they had suffered their first bombardment, they tended to disparage it as a weapon. They threw away their masks—"lost them"—because they were a nuisance to carry; they joked, yelling "gas!", for example, when someone nearby broke wind; and some of the officers punished their men by making them perform calisthenics while wearing their masks. The division paid dearly for this cavalier attitude: over three-quarters of its gas casualties suffered in the entire war occurred in the month of June. After Belleau Wood the men were more prudent, more respectful of the invisible killer—but by then, for nearly a thousand of them, it was too late.

THE first gas attack came on the night of June 13-14 when the Germans saturated Lucy-le-Bocage and the southern half of Belleau Wood with seven thousand mustard gas bombs and a couple of thousand high-explosive shells that contained ten per cent of diphenylarsine. The purpose of the bombardment was to interdict both Belleau Wood and the approaches to it to the Allies, and to allow Corps Conta to advance to the defensive positions it had selected on June 4. Even to a casual student of the battle this seems obvious, for French observation planes had reported heavy circulation of troops and guns behind the enemy lines for several days previous to the bombardment. But French and American intelligence ignored these clear signs of impending attack and said simply: "From the indiscriminate use of mustard gas it would appear that the object of the enemy is merely to cause losses and not to prepare for immediate attack." The only satisfactory explanation for this curious interpretation of the facts is that the intelligence services were, so to speak, whistling in the dark, so apprehensive of another drive toward Paris that they preferred not to consider the real meaning of this gas bombardment.

The bombardment coincided with a general readjustment of the 2nd Division's lines. To remove some of the pressure from the exhausted marine brigade, for which he was still unable to obtain relief, General Bundy had arranged to shorten its sector. Major Elliott's battalion of the 23rd was to take over the defense of Bouresches, and General Degoutte had agreed that the 167th Division should extend its line to the right and occupy the marines' positions on Hill 142. This was Degoutte's last official act as commander of the XXI Corps, for he was promoted to command of the Sixth French Army, relieving General Duchesne, and his place was taken by General Naulin. As part of this readjustment, which had the code name APPOMATTOX, Major Holcomb's battalion was to relieve Colonel Wise's. The timing was unfortunate, for Holcomb's men were making their way through the southern half of Belleau Wood when the bombardment began.

As the gas bombs burst with their distinctive plopping sound, easily distinguished from the high-explosive shells that were also falling, the battalion dissolved from an organized body of troops into a terrified mob. It was a dark, overcast night and, even without their masks on, the men could hardly see where they were going. With them on, they were totally blind. They blundered about in the blackness, knocking their masks off against trees, tearing their clothes and flesh on twigs and brambles, falling into shell holes, crawling along the ground in a mad search for shelter. The diphenylarsine had got to many of them before the alarm was given, and soon they were ripping off their masks with frantic fingers, retching violently, and sucking in great lungfuls of the deadly mustard vapor. A few of the old-time leathernecks kept their heads and tried to restore some semblance of order and lead the wounded to the battalion dressing station. One of them, Gunnery Sergeant Fred Stockham, won the division's second Medal of Honor by putting his own mask on the face of a man wounded by shrapnel and by continuing to help the other wounded until he collapsed, dying a few days later.

Holcomb's battalion had been eight hundred strong, including recently arrived replacements, when it started out to relieve Colonel Wise. At three o'clock in the morning the survivors of the gas attack, about three hundred men, began drifting into his post of command. "I did not consider that they were sufficient to relieve me," the colonel reported laconically, "and remained in position."

- There was a few hours' respite for the Americans, then, at 4:30 P.M. on the 14th, the Germans once again bombarded the woods with mustard gas. Both Major Hughes's battalion and a battalion of the 23rd suffered heavily. Hughes himself was evacuated with severely burned eyes, as were the two doctors in charge of his battalion dressing station. The casualties in the 23rd were caused largely by the carelessness or ignorance of a company commander. Shortly after the bombardment stopped, he calmly sat down on the stump of a tree and took off his mask. His men naturally assumed that it was safe to do the same—and over a hundred and fifty of them, including the captain, were evacuated with damaged lungs and bad burns about the body. Other casualties occurred when men in dugouts removed their masks prematurely: they supposed, wrongly, that the gas could not pass the blankets and shelter-halves that were draped before the entrances.

A third bombardment, on the morning of June 15, brought the total of gas casualties to over eight hundred, most of them in the marine brigade. The Germans had achieved their purpose: Harbord was forced to evacuate the woods completely except for a narrow strip along the eastern edge, which he held with machine guns. This left the northern and western sections of the wood open to infiltration, though neither Harbord nor Bundy seemed to realize this until several days later. The Germans did realize it—but could not take advantage of it, for Corps Conta was in a bad way. The entire 237th Division had been reduced to less than fifteen hundred men, and many of these were unfit for combat. Indeed, on June 14 the commanding general ordered all office work suspended and put the clerks, signal men, orderlies, and other rear-echelon troops into the line. Nor were the 5th Guard and 28th Infantry in much better shape. The 28th especially had been badly mauled. On June 19 it reported: "The severe losses and the many cases of sickness of the past few weeks have further diminished the combat value of the division." The worn troops had to remain in the front line, however, for General von Conta had no fresh ones with which to replace them.

It was now imperative that the marine brigade be relieved at once. It had been reduced to about half-strength, and the survivors were so near exhaustion that "they moved like sleepwalkers . . . black hollows under their eyes, a dirty stubble on their chins, their uniforms sticking to their bodies." Bundy tried once more to get some action from A.E.F. headquarters, reporting to Pershing: "It is well known that the moral effect of the success of American arms on this front has been great. To jeopardize that success by the continued service in the front line of a weakened division might have a serious turn. If the division could be placed south of the Marne for a short period of rest and reorganization, it would reenter the line with renewed vigor." There is no record of Pershing's reply to this rather weakly worded request, but it must have been unfavorable for, on the 15th, Bundy went with the same request to the corps commander, General Naulin.

At first Naulin said there was nothing he could do. He suggested that Bundy spread out the 3rd Brigade along the entire division front and use the marines as reserves. Bundy refused to consider this, saying the front was far too unstable to take the risk. Then he pointed out that the 3rd American Division was in Army reserve a few miles to the south; why not let him have one of its brigades, at least for a few days? Naulin reluctantly agreed to this proposal, and so the 7th Infantry Brigade relieved the marine brigade for six days, beginning June 15. The relief took place on three successive nights, a battalion at a time, and all the heavy equipment—machine guns, mortars, water and ammunition carts, kitchens, etc.—was temporarily exchanged so that there would be little movement for the Germans to observe.

Colonel Wise's battalion was relieved on the night of the 15th, and shortly after dawn the next morning his troops assembled near a farmhouse some two miles behind the lines. Wise and his one remaining company commander, Captain Lester Wass (killed a couple of months later), lined them up and looked them over. "It was enough to break your heart," Wise wrote. "I had left

Courcelles [a village near Chaumont-en-Vexin] on May 31 with 965 men and 26 officers. Now, before me, stood 350 men and 6 officers—615 men and 19 officers gone. For 17 days they hadn't had a cup of hot coffee or a bite of hot food. They hadn't taken off their shoes. They hadn't had a chance to wash their faces. Even drinking water had been scarce for days. Their only rest had been on bare ground. For the last four days they had even been without packs. . . . They had driven trained German veterans out of fortified positions by frontal attack; had walked into the fiercest kind of woods fighting in France; had taken nearly twice their own number in German prisoners, and captured more than 50 machine guns and half a dozen trench mortars. They had made a record never surpassed in the war."

Everything Wise wrote was true. He should have added, however, that Belleau Wood, in the most literal meaning of the words, was still No Man's Land.

CHAPTER 11

IT seemed hardly possible that the battle for the woods could continue at the intense pitch of the past two weeks. No matter how important that kidney-shaped patch of forest had become as a symbol, no matter the psychological effects of its capture or loss, surely flesh and blood could do no more. Indeed, the symbol itself had been mauled and battered beyond recognition. Most of the trees looked as though they had been struck by lightning. Lines of rusting barbed wire ran crazily this way and that, with here and there a body or part of a body hanging from it. Entire systems of trenches had been pounded into sandy ruin by the thousands of artillery shells that had fallen on them. A poisonous miasma of mustard gas clung to the hollows, making passage difficult, if not impossible. And everywhere the dead lay in the grotesque attitudes in which they had fallen.

Nevertheless the commanding generals on each side were more than ever determined that Belleau Wood must be taken and held, no matter what the cost. The battle had assumed the proportions of a crusade, a contest of national wills; it was, the commanders seemed to feel, the war itself in microcosm, and they attached a superstitious significance to its outcome.

The struggle had begun with the Americans on the defense and the Germans on the offense. These positions were now reversed, for Corps Conta had been ordered "temporarily" to assume the defensive while preparations were made to renew the assault elsewhere against less stubborn opposition. The 87th Division relieved the depleted 237th; the 28th's line was shortened in lieu of giving the troops a much-needed rest; and all positions were organized in depth. Under no circumstances, the men of the 87th were told, were they to relinquish their hold on the northern lobe of the woods.

The Americans could not resume the assault until the 7th Brigade became thoroughly familiar with its new surroundings or until the marines returned to the front, but they maintained constant pressure on the Germans with artillery, machine guns, and patrols. The following patrol report, chosen at random from many similar reports, will suffice to give the full flavor of these nightly operations:

Patrol report, 9th Infantry, June 15. (Confidential, not to be taken into the front lines.)

Composition of patrol: Lieutenant William Zwicky, Battalion Scout Officer, 1st Battalion; three sergeants, one corporal, five privates.

Mission: to capture enemy sentinel in wood at point which patrol commander had located in reconnaissance of June 12. (Map issued very inaccurate.)

Patrol left junction of Paris road and road running northwest of Bourbelin at 10:50 P.M., taking course along road where it reaches the woods. From this point the patrol crawled on open plowed ground along the edge of the woods and through open ground to the trail. The going in No Man's Land was fair but progress was slow, as patrol kept very close to the ground in crawling. Patrol reached the trail after about 45 minutes of crawling, and continued along it to where it joined the road. At this point it was halted and lay in skirmish line facing point at which the sentinel had been previously located. Violent artillery bombardment on both sides but no shells in this area. Between shells the voices of two or more Germans were heard from the suspected point about twelve yards from where the patrol lay. Leaving two sergeants and five privates in this position, patrol leader took remaining sergeant and corporal and crawled along northwest edge of woods to distance of about a hundred yards. Got through underbrush and out on main road. Patrol leader and non-coms walked from this point, patrol leader on left side of road going towards outpost, non-coms on right side. Immediately after crossing the road, patrol leader observed one enemy cross from right to left side of road, and after about a minute return to the right side. Patrol did not hesitate but pushed on as quietly as possible. When within five yards of the enemy, a twig cracked beneath patrol commander's feet. Enemy called: *"Halt! Ver da?"* Patrol leader, who speaks German, called the same thing at the same time, then said: *"Er gibt euch!"* Enemy called *"Halt!"* again. Patrol leader commanded: *"Hande Hoch!"* One enemy fired two shots from rifle and another shot at the patrol leader. Leader dropped prone at the first shot. After third shot he opened fire with automatic pistol. While enemy continued to fire, both using their rifles, sergeant and corporal opened fire with their rifles and both enemy dropped. Immediately patrol leader called reserve of two sergeants and five privates who were lying about twelve yards from this spot. They had been ordered to hold places and not rush in until called, in order to prevent mixup of our own men in the dark. Reserve party, at order of patrol leader, dragged body of one enemy to spot previously designated for rendezvous. Patrol commander with two companions immediately searched the other body. This man had no blouse or coat and only a blanket over his white shirt. His pockets were empty. His body was thoroughly searched, even his boots. His helmet bore the name Sofsky. About six feet two inches tall, 175 pounds, 32 years old. Small dark mustache. No I.D. tags found;

no markings on bayonet scabbard. Patrol leader joined rest of patrol at rendezvous. Other body clothed in jacket bearing numerals 444 on shoulder strap. A piece of paper in which a package had evidently been sent him from his wife, was found in his right coat sleeve. It bore the address: "Defr. Neumann, 6th Company, 2nd Battalion, 444 Regiment." His pocketbook was so full of coagulating blood that the papers were not removed for fear of tearing them. Pocketbook contained *soldbuch* [paybook], some letters. Neumann also had a blanket. He was a man about forty years old, weight about 180, black mustache. Gas mask, shoulder strap, button from coat, pocketbook and other identification was promptly forwarded to G2, 2nd Division. Patrol left body at point of rendezvous as it was in a very bad condition from wounds and too heavy to carry, and reentered our lines at point of exit at 1:45 A.M. Behavior of patrol excellent, especially reserve group in lying still when they saw officer fall and thought he had been killed.

William Zwicky (signed)

At least ten or fifteen patrols went out every night from both the German and the American lines. Some of them were larger than Lieutenant Zwicky's and their purpose was simply to kill as many of the enemy as possible. Both sides were kept at a high pitch of tension and fear by these roving groups, and, considering that no heavy attacks took place for over a week, there was a disquieting number of casualties and cases of combat fatigue.

CORPS CONTA had captured seventy-odd marines, as well as a few soldiers from the less active 3rd Brigade, during the fighting for the woods. They were interrogated separately and collectively, both to learn whatever military information of value they might possess and to form an estimate of their quality as soldiers. On June 16 the corps commander issued an evaluation report, which was sent to all his division commanders. The report offers a good insight into both the Americans and their captors. It reads: "The 2nd American Division can be rated as a very good division if not quite as an assault division. The various attacks with both of the marine regiments were carried out with vigor and without consideration of losses. Morale effect of our firearms did not materially check the advance of the infantry. The nerve of the Americans is still unshaken. They may be considered excellent personnel. They are healthy, strong, physically well set-up men from 18 to 28 years old, who at present only lack the necessary training to make them a dangerous foe. The spirit of the troops is high and they possess an innocent self-confidence. The characteristic expression of the prisoners is 'We kill or get killed.' In general they present a wide-awake agreeable impression, but they seem entirely uninterested in military things. They were intentionally kept ignorant of certain things by their superiors. Most of them had never seen a map and were unable to designate villages or roads over which they had marched. They have many hazy ideas relative to the distribution of their ogranization. One prisoner insisted that his brigade had six regiments and his division twenty-four. They still view the war with the attitude of a 'big brother' who is coming to help his distressed sister and who is received with a glad hand wherever he goes. The majority of the prisoners add, with natural innocence, that they came to Europe to defend their country. Only a few of them, by ancestry, are real Americans. The majority are of German, Dutch or Italian parentage. Still, these half-Americans, who without exception were born in America and who never before set foot in Europe, consider themselves genuine sons of America."

Even in translation there is both a patronizing air and an underlying querulousness to this report. The patronizing air needs no explanation: it is typically German, and shows their contempt for all things and people non-Germanic, and especially for the "half-breed" Americans. The querulousness can be directly traced to the tremor of shock and indignation that went through Germany when America entered the war. Such an act was contrary to German notions of *realpolitik*. The United States, after all, was not a member of the British Commonwealth and, beyond a certain vague emotional connection, she had no ties to France. Why, then, was she sending her young men to fight three thousand miles from home? It was incomprehensible—and a bitter pill indeed to swallow, for with Russia knocked out and Italy nearly so, the Central Powers had had the war as good as won. Despite the strong mystical and transcendental elements in their own natures, the Germans never did understand the Americans' romantic sympathy for the underdog, or their dislike—which was easily whipped up into hatred—of the nation that had violated Belgian neutrality, sunk the "Lusitania," and introduced flame throwers and poison gas into the war. The Germans felt they had been stabbed in the back, and their indignation turned querulous when America's troops demonstrated an unanticipated high quality.

MAJOR ELLIOTT'S battalion of the 23rd took over the marines' positions in Bouresches on June 14. "This town is the most messed up place I've ever seen," one of the company commanders reported shortly after moving in. "Dead cows, Boche, cats, and most anything lying around. The streets are full of debris, and what's left of the houses is a grand mess of household goods strewn everywhere, mingled with china, vegetables, and what-not. . . . The marines left enough property to outfit a regiment."

The infantry had no plans to attack but concentrated on repairing and extending the system of trenches on the eastern and southern edges of the village. The troops had to work during the six hours of darkness, for German artillery and machine guns were active in daylight hours and immediately opened fire at any signs of movement. Nevertheless, compared to the activity of the past two weeks, it was a quiet period, and most of the messages that flew back and forth among the various headquarters concerned the quality of the food. Captain William Moore, commanding I Company, waxed especially loquacious in his complaints, some of which ran to two pages. He griped about "marmites" of spoiled beef and beans, about coffee in dirty cans, rotten tomatoes, lack of salt and pepper, etc. When these reports reached the regimental commander, he sent a Lieutenant Swink into the village to look things over, and Swink reported that the troops were "nicely situated." This enraged Moore. "I can't say

I agree entirely with Lieutenant Swink's estimate of the situation down here," he wrote to Major Elliott. "During the last three days we have killed a couple of beeves, but, alas, had no salt, so they were not all that could be desired. The only way to make out on chow at all is due to the fact that I found some canned meat, French issue, left by marines, and some potatoes in a couple of the cellars. . . . Lieutenant Swink happened to be here on a quiet day and night. Please extend my invitation to anyone at H.Q. who feels so inclined to pay a little visit. I do not consider that it is physically or mentally possible for men to stand any more than the men of this company have stood. If they consider: having a town completely demolished overhead, suffering twelve to fifteen per cent casualties, not having sufficient food, previously having a hundred to five hundred shells dropped on you every day and night, having to sneak and gumshoe everywhere you go, running across spaces open to observation, being sniped at constantly, having to remain under cover when not actually on post in places that are not shellproof. To be covered with lice and fleas and to be under the mental and physical strain that the men are under. If they call that 'nicely situated' I would like some of them to try a shift at it!"

Captain Bruce, whose company of marine machine gunners had not been relieved with the rest of the 4th Brigade, asked that an official complaint be lodged against the YMCA representative attached to the division. He had distributed chocolate, cigarettes, and newspapers to the infantry free of charge, Bruce said, while the marines were asked to pay for the same items. With few exceptions, the YMCA representatives were not popular with either the troops or the French. (Their counterparts in the Knights of Columbus, a more rough and ready lot, were popular.) Their "churchly" manner and frequent lectures on the "evils of the flesh" irritated the troops. Then, too, there was evidently a number of hypocrites among them, for the French prostitutes referred to them as " 'Y'a Moyen Coucher Avec."

Major Elliott, too, had his complaints. (It seems likely, from the following message, that after the fiasco on June 6 the major was regarded with some apprehension by his superiors.) The message, which he sent to 23rd Regiment headquarters on June 20, read: "As some of the requests, orders and reports of some of the staff are so absurd, ludicrous and in many cases impossible, I request that the following officers visit my post of command to see the situation for themselves: Regimental Gas Officer, Regimental Information Officer, Regimental Signal Officer, Regimental Surgeon. For instance, to receive instructions that no one will sleep within 1,200 yards of the front lines, unless in a gas-proof dugout with gas sentries over each dugout, would keep all of us awake all of the time. Another thing: that a man who is exposed to mustard gas should have a warm bath with soap and a change of clothing, when as a matter of fact we don't get enough water to wash regularly and some of the men are about to fall through their clothes, even though requisitions were submitted some time ago. . . . It becomes exasperating to receive so many orders and requests which someone has doped out of a book and from the maps. Another thing they should remember is that the *actual defense* of this position must be considered and that it takes some time each day."

From the nature and length of these messages it is evident that things were fairly quiet in Bouresches: men busy fighting have no time for minor complaints. Indeed, things were so quiet that Captain Moore sent a note concerning an event that would have passed unnoticed a few days earlier. "I am sending you the I.D. tags taken off a Boche killed the night before last," he wrote to Elliott. "We brought him in last night and buried him eight feet deep in a manure pile."

THE 7th Brigade meanwhile had been hard at work in and around Belleau Wood. The 2nd Battalion wired in the east face of the woods in preparation for a German attack, should one come (the Germans had no such intentions); the 3rd Battalion "rectified" its lines with no opposition; the 1st Battalion, however, under Lieutenant Colonel John Adams, probed the German main line of resistance and recoiled with twenty casualties. On the morning of June 20 this battalion tried to envelop and crowd out the Germans without a formal attack, but made no headway. Harbord ordered the battalion to try again the following morning, still with no artillery preparation. "Your battalion will be relieved tomorrow night," he wrote to Colonel Adams. "Tomorrow morning is its only chance to redeem failure made this morning. If you clear the northern half of the Bois de Belleau the credit will belong to the 1st Battalion, 7th Infantry, and will be freely given. The battalion cannot afford to fail again."

Colonel Adams was so perturbed when he received these orders that he sent the following extraordinary message to Harbord: "Information has reached me that the Germans have filtered through and have in place at least fifteen machine guns in and around Belleau Wood. [They had in fact more than fifty, manned by three companies of the 87th Division.] They are now firing into the rear of Companies D and C and have moved two guns up toward the right flank of Company B. Under the conditions noted, I do not believe any attack without a heavy artillery fire preceding can remove the guns from the woods. They are all emplaced and strongly held. The woods is almost a thicket and the throwing of troops into them is filtering away men with nothing gained. . . . I can assure you that the orders to attack will stand as given, but it cannot succeed. This is only my individual expression and has not reached the ears of anyone else. . . ."

Harbord was somewhat taken aback by this criticism of his plan, but he agreed to order several batteries of artillery to fire on the target area from 2:00 A.M. until 3:30 A.M., when the troops were scheduled to move out. Despite these changes, the attack, as Colonel Adams had foreseen, was a failure. One company was all but wiped out by the German machine guns, and the battalion lost almost two hundred men before it fell back to the jump-off line. One reason for the failure was that apparently some of the Germans had fought in American uniforms. Colonel Anderson, the 7th's commander (who acted in an advisory capacity during the brigade's period in the woods), investigated the situation just after the attack and was told by several of his officers that groups of Germans in American uniforms fired on the infantry. "At one point in the attack," Anderson reported to Harbord, "when the line had engaged the enemy, a German in American uniform approached Lieutenant Paysley, Company A, saying: 'My God! You're not going to fire on your own men out there in front, are you?' Paysley [killed the following night] immediately spotted him for a German and shot and killed him, in the excitement of the moment not obtaining insignia or identification from the body. . . ." Paysley was the chief witness, and he died before a further investigation could be made, so the question was never resolved. Had the Germans fought in American uniforms, or had some men of another unit accidentally crossed Company A's line of fire? The latter seems the likeliest possibility, for the affair was quickly hushed up.

Another reason for the failure of the attack was the suspect behavior of the officer in command of the company that suffered the heaviest losses. This lieutenant turned up at the headquarters of another battalion a couple of hours after the assault had begun, claiming to have been stunned by a hand grenade and to have lost his way. Harbord investigated personally and reported to division headquarters that "this officer has no marks of any kind on himself or his clothing. The post of command at which he reported is a full kilometer west of where he claims to have been stunned, and in the opposite direction from his company. . . ."

The main reason the attack failed, however, was that the German defenses were too strong to be overcome by one battalion—at least by one battalion of untried infantry. Perhaps the marines, who were returning to the line that night and who were now excessively familiar with woods fighting, would prove more successful.

CHAPTER 12

AT eleven o'clock Saturday night, June 22, Privates Byington and Clumber, both former Tennessee mule skinners, were making their regular delivery of rations to a battalion of the 23rd Infantry just south of Belleau Wood.

It was cool and cloudy and they had wrapped blankets around their shoulders as the mules slowly pulled the ration cart along the road. They had used the same route at the same time for the past week, ever since the 7th Brigade had relieved the marines, and had had no trouble from German artillery. But now, as the mules topped a small rise, shells began exploding nearby and the men could hear the hiss of shrapnel passing all around them. The mules chose this moment to balk. Byington broke a general order and beat them furiously with the ends of the reins, but they still refused to budge. The shells were coming more thickly now, and closer, so the two men jumped off the cart and took cover in the ditch alongside the road. "All right, you bastards," Byington called to the mules. "Stay there and get killed. I don't aim to!" Then he turned to Private Clumber and said, "Right quiet for a week—and now this. Reckon them goddam marines is back in the line!"

The marines were indeed back in the line—somewhat rested by their six days in a relatively peaceful area near the village of Mery, with an additional eight hundred replacements (which still left them far short of full strength), and determined to clean out Belleau Wood, once and for all.

Major Shearer's battalion of the 5th took over Colonel Adams' positions on the night of June 21 and immediately stirred things up by sending out reconnaissance and combat patrols. Early the following morning one of these patrols brought an Alsatian deserter into Shearer's post of command. He was taken to division headquarters and questioned by Colonel Brown. Eager to be of help, he marked out the German main line of resistance on a map. It ran through the northern part of the woods several hundred yards south of the edge. There had been some doubt of this in headquarters, for Colonel Feland, in overall charge of the troops in the woods, had said that the enemy held only the extreme northern tip, although the rest of that section was wide open to infiltration. Reporting on this new development to Gernal Bundy, Harbord wrote: "The undersigned [himself] has been misled as to affairs in that end of the woods, either consciously or unconsciously, ever since its first occupation by the battalion under command of Lieutenant Colonel F. M. Wise. . . ."

"Consciously or unconsciously"—these strong words, which practically accused Colonel Wise of cowardice or treachery, were the result of a meeting between Harbord and Wise shortly after the marines had been relieved by the 7th Infantry. Unfortunately we have only Wise's account of the meeting, which took place on June 16 in Harbord's office in La Loge Farm.

" 'Twice you reported to me that those woods were clear of Germans, when they weren't,' " Wise records Harbord as saying.

" 'I did—but the minute I found out the error by personal inspection, you were notified.'

"He himself had reported the woods cleared and had had to backfire on it. My nerves were stretched pretty taut after eighteen days. I blew up. 'If you had so much doubt about those woods being cleared, why the hell didn't someone from Brigade come out and take a look?' I don't remember exactly what I did say after that. It must have been plenty. . . ."

It must have been plenty indeed, for it put an effective end to Wise's career in the Marine Corps. He was sent back to a hospital to "rest his nerves," and the battalion was taken over by Major Ralph Keyser, his second in command. Wise retired in 1926—still with the rank of lieutenant colonel. . . .

Harbord's report to General Bundy went on to say that Major Shearer, "now in there, has been told that this is intolerable and that he will clean the woods by ten o'clock tomorrow night; further, that the space does not permit the use of more troops than he now has and that it is not practicable to make artillery preparation by withdrawing his troops. . . ."

The attack began at 7:00 P.M. on June 23 after a short and thoroughly ineffective preparatory barrage by Stokes mortars and machine guns. It was a repetition in miniature of all the previous attacks—with one added disadvantage: the ground was too rocky for the marines to dig in under fire. They used the same tactics as before— bombing the machine-gun nests with hand grenades, then charging with fixed bayonets and firing from the hip—and failed completely. "The farthest advance made was about twenty yards," Major Shearer reported late that night, "to the top of the rocks near the 'Hook' sector. This position was immediately made untenable by machine gun fire. This company gained no ground to the front that could be held and are now in original position. Three outposts have been established in front of old position. Sniping from these positions is being successfully carried out. The enemy seems to have unlimited alternate gun positions and many guns, each gun position covered by others. I know of no other way of attacking these positions with better chance of success than one attempted, and am of the opinion that infantry alone cannot dislodge the enemy guns. Water is difficult to obtain, rations scarce. Men and officers very tired but retain their spirit."

AN anonymous manuscript history of the 2nd Division at Château-Thierry contains the following astute paragraph: ". . . It may be said in a general way that the real way to deal with a position of this sort [Belleau Wood] was by gas bombardment. The total area of the wood is small; it was isolated from the next supporting enemy position; and however strongly held with rifles and machine guns its resisting power could have been reduced to almost nothing by a mustard preparation of a few hours. But the trouble was that there was no mustard gas available. The Division had been rushed in; its artillery had been gotten up some hours before in the same sort of scramble; and the obtaining of any sort of munitions for the artillery had come about merely through the energy of the command. The Division as a fighting unit was not equipped for dealing with the problem of the Belleau Wood. The thing had therefore resolved itself into almost a straight infantry proposition, which it should not have been."

It was still a "straight infantry proposition," for the German machine guns in the northern lobe stuck in the marines' throats like a bone. It was, as Harbord had told Shearer, "intolerable," and on the morning of June 24 he called a conference with the division commanders, the artillery commanders, and the commanders of the 5th Marines to see what could be done about it.

There was a strong undercurrent of tension at the meeting. For one thing, everyone present felt that the culmination of the battle was now at hand, that one last massive effort would carry the enemy positions and completely clear the woods. And for another thing, Harbord's and Bundy's mutual dislike was now so strong that they addressed one another with excessive formality and politeness and made everyone else uncomfortable. "Everybody recognized that the 4th Brigade needed rest," Harbord wrote later. "The 3rd had not been so actively engaged. Neither had the 3rd Brigade had the opportunity to distinguish itself as had the 4th. As early as the 20th of June we knew informally that if the division commander, Bundy, would ask it, a division would relieve us. [This was probably true: Bundy's requests were very weakly worded and never stressed the urgent need for this relief.] For some reason he would not ask it. I could not convince the marines that it wasn't because he wouldn't leave until the 3rd Brigade had also had a chance to 'pull off a stunt.'" (It is obvious that Harbord had by now thoroughly identified himself with his brigade and was, as Colonel Catlin had said, as "pro-marine as any marine." Bundy's dislike (read "jealousy") of Harbord culminated in an act of magnificent pettiness on June 27. Clemenceau paid a visit to the division to congratulate it for its splendid fight, and the commanding officers of all the brigades were invited to meet him—of all the brigades, that is, except the 4th. Harbord was not informed of the Premier's visit until the following day! . . .

At the conference it was decided to call upon the artillery once more. In previous attacks the heavy guns had had a fairly large target to bombard, as well as the German batteries behind Torcy and Bussiares, and consequently their fire had been somewhat scattered and ineffective. Now the target was only a couple of hundred yards in extent. The guns could pour a concentrated fire into it and perhaps kill and stun enough Germans to facilitate the marines' advance. Also, previous barrages had been short and intense. This one was scheduled to

136

last fourteen hours, from 3:00 A.M. to 5:00 P.M., when Major Shearer's battalion would go over the top.

Saturation shelling by the enemy was the one tactic Major Bischoff had feared above all others; it was, he had known, the only way in which the natural defensive advantages of the woods could be overcome. Now he was proved correct. Hour after hour the 155's, 75's, and 105's rained down into the northern end of the woods, shattering the remaining trees, riddling the walls and trophies of the hunting lodge with shrapnel, plowing great holes in the ground, and sending branches and jagged chunks of metal crashing down on the heads of the Germans cowering in their trenches and dugouts. It was the heaviest and most concentrated bombardment of the battle, and it performed its deadly work well, for those Germans who were not killed or wounded by the shells were left dazed and shaken and able to put up only token resistance to the advancing marines.

A couple of hours before the attack started, General Harbord's sergeant major asked the general's permission to go to the front and "get a little experience." The sergeant major was in line for a commission but was reluctant to accept it without seeing some action and without doing a preliminary term at the officers' candidate school, although Harbord had the authority to appoint a number of second lieutenants in the field. Harbord reluctantly gave his consent, for he was fond of the sergeant major, and he told him not to take any chances. The sergeant major reported to Shearer and was given command of a platoon. . . . Four days later his body was found in the woods, torn by high-explosive fragments. "Thus ended the career of Sergeant Major William J. Geary," wrote Harbord, "Headquarters Detachment, 4th Brigade, Virginian."

Geary's ardor was matched or exceeded by the worn troops in Shearer's battalion. Not only did they sense that the battle was in its final phase and gird themselves up accordingly, but they knew that once the woods had been taken they could expect to be relieved. So they attacked with a verve that had not been seen since June 6, taking one machine gun after another, capturing over four hundred prisoners, and driving the remaining Germans beyond the railroad embankment east of Torcy and the village of Belleau.

At nine-twenty the following morning Pilot-Observer Villaret of Esquadrille Squadron 252, returning from his daily reconnaissance of the woods, sent a message to Colonel Malone of the 23rd Infantry: "The Bois de Belleau has been cleared of the enemy. . . . Quiet here now."

It was the quiet of the grave, for 5,199 officers and men of the Marine Brigade had been killed or wounded in and around its shattered trees.

With Army Staff   Army H.Q., June 30, 1918

ORDER

In view of the brilliant conduct of the 4th Brigade of the 2nd U.S. Division, which in a spirited fight took Bouresches and the important strong point of Belleau Wood, stubbornly defended by a large enemy force, the General commanding the Sixth Army orders that henceforth, in all official papers, the Bois de Belleau shall be named "Bois de la Brigade de Marine."

Division General Degoutte
Commanding Sixth Army
Degoutte (signed)

EPILOGUE

EVEN at this remove it is difficult to form a just estimate of the Battle of Belleau Wood. It is still a controversial subject among historians and among veterans of the war. "The Gettysburg of this war has been fought," General Pershing said to General Bundy and Colonel Brown early in July. At the time this was a view shared by many Americans, and, indeed, at first glance there are several parallels between the two battles. Both were won by the "right" side; both were fought by brigades rather than by larger units; and both were the scene of enormous casualties. But there the parallels end, for the crucial comparison will not hold water: Gettysburg was the turning point of the Civil War, and Belleau Wood was most decidedly *not* the turning point of the First World War.

It was also claimed at the time that the marines had "saved Paris." On July 1 General Bliss wrote to General Pershing: "Frequently remarks have been made to me by French officers of all ranks, by French civilians, and by my British colleagues, plainly expressing their belief that the American troops in the vicinity of Château-Thierry stopped the German drive and very possibly saved Paris."

In 1956 another view was taken by General Matthew Ridgway. He described Belleau Wood as "one of many prize examples of men's lives being thrown away against objectives which were not worth the cost . . . a monument, for all time, to the inflexibility of military thinking in that period."

There is something to be said for each point of view. As a purely military objective, Belleau Wood was certainly not worth its cost in killed and wounded. A mustard-gas bombardment, as has been pointed out, could have driven the Germans out within a day or two at little or no cost in Allied lives. But as a "psychological" objective, Belleau Wood was something else entirely. If the marines did not actually "save Paris"—and this is by no means certain—they did other things that were perhaps as important. They stood fast when the French were retreating on all sides; they convincingly demonstrated to our dubious allies that American troops were the equal of any in the war; they rendered easier Pershing's task of forming an independent American Army in the face of Clemenceau's and Lloyd George's determined opposition; and, by no means least, they caused five German divisions to be declared "unfit for further combat" by their commanding officers. This is not a record to be ashamed of, no matter the blunders of the commanding generals. For sheer viciousness of fighting, Belleau Wood ranks with Guadalcanal, Iwo Jima, and the other island campaigns of the Second World War, and the battle has a secure place in the pantheon of Marine Corps' victories. As General Harbord wrote several years later—and this could well stand as the epitaph of the battle: "Insignificant in area, not especially picturesque, out of the ordinary track of travel and with no particular traditions of peace or of earlier wars—the accident of place and the chance stroke of a zero hour wrote the name of Belleau Wood on the records."

BIBLIOGRAPHY

The primary source for the book was the boxed records of the
2nd Division in the National Archives in Washington, D.C. I
have also consulted many periodicals of the day, especially the
New York *Times,* but since these are referred to by name
throughout the book they are not listed here.

Aston, George, *Marshal Foch.* Macmillan, New York, 1929.

Blunden, Edmund, *Undertones of War.* Doubleday Doran, New
York, 1929.

Brophy, Leo P., Miles, Wyndham D., and Cochrane, Rexmond C.,
From Laboratory to Field. Office of Chief of Military History,
1959.

Bullard, Robert Lee, *American Soldiers Also Fought.* Longmans,
Green and Co., New York, 1936.

Bullard, Robert Lee, *Personalities and Reminiscences of the War.*
Doubleday, Page and Co., New York, 1925.

Catlin, A. W., *With the Help of God and a Few Marines.* Doubleday, Page and Co., New York, 1919.

Cowing, Kemper F. (compiled by), *Dear Folks at Home.*
Houghton-Mifflin Co., Boston, 1919.

Derby, Richard, *Wade in, Sanitary!.* G. P. Putnam's Sons, New
York, 1919.

Fredericks, Pierce G., *The Great Adventure.* E. P. Dutton and
Co., New York, 1960.

Gibbons, Floyd, *And They Thought We Wouldn't Fight.* George
H. Doran Co., New York, 1918.

Graves, Robert, *Goodbye to All That.* Doubleday Anchor Books,
second revised edition, New York, 1957.

Harbord, James G., *Leaves from a War Diary.* Dodd, Mead and
Co., New York, 1925.

Harbord, James G., *The American Army in France.* Little, Brown
and Co., Boston, 1936.

Ludendorff, Erich von, *The American Effort. Atlantic Monthly,*
May, 1922.

Muzzey, David Saville, *The United States of America,* vol. II.
Ginn and Co., Boston, 1937.

O'Connor, Richard, *Black Jack Pershing*. Doubleday and Co., New York, 1961.

Palmer, Frederick, *Bliss, Peacemaker*. Dodd, Mead and Co., New York, 1934.

Pattullo, George, *Horrors of Moonlight*. Allston and Depew, New York, 1939.

Pershing, John J., *My Experiences in the World War*. Frederick A. Stokes Co., New York, 1931.

Pierrefeu, Jean de, *From French H.Q. 1915 to 1918*. Geoffrey Bles, London, 1924.

Pottle, Frederick A., *Stretchers*. Yale University Press, 1929.

Rendinell, J. E., and Patullo, George, *One Man's War*. J. H. Sears and Co., New York, 1928.

Shipley, Thomas, *The History of the A.E.F.* George H. Doran Co., New York, 1920.

Thomason, John W., Jr., *Fix Bayonets*. Charles Scribner's Sons, New York, 1925.

Westover, Wendell, *Suicide Battalions*. G. P. Putnam's Sons, New York, 1929.

Wise, Frederic May, *A Marine Tells It to You*. J. H. Sears and Co., New York, 1929.

In addition I made frequent reference to the following anonymous or collective works:

Americans Defending Democracy. World War Stories, Inc., New York, 1919.

The Second Division, Historical Committee of the Second Division Association: The Hillman Press, Inc., New York, 1937.

U.S. Army Chemical Corps Historical Studies, *Gas Warfare at Belleau Wood*. 1957.

Wine, Women and War. J. H. Sears and Co., New York, 1926.

INDEX

Adams, John, Colonel, 131, 133
Adriatic Fleet, 31
Alsace, 9, 12
American Expeditionary Force, 1, 4, 9, 94; headquarters, 17, 60, 92, 110
American troops, British and French objection to use of, 4–7, 8–11; French distrust of, 43
Amiens, 7, 12, 32, 97
Anderson, Colonel, 131–132
Anderson, George (fictitious), 82–89
Annamites, 18
"Arkansas Pete," 19–20
Austria, 31

Baker, Newton D., 6
Balfour, Arthur, 29
Barnett, Major General, 39, 76
Battle of the Bulge, 13
Bayonet, French ("Rosalie"), 49
Bayonet, saw-toothed, 49
Beauvais, 17
Belfry, Earl, Private, 74
Belgium, 7, 8, 49, 128
Belleau (village), 44, 47, 52, 138
Belleau Wood, 14, 44, 47 ff; description of site, 47
Berlin, 2
Bernsdorff, von, 51
Berry, Benjamin, Major, 48, 61–66, 67, 72, 77–79, 113
"Big Berthas," 2, 94
Bischoff, Major, 49–51, 64, 69, 70, 72, 99, 100, 101, 105, 137
"Black Jack," 4; see also Pershing
Blanchfield, John, Captain, 78
Bliss, General, 11, 30, 31, 139

Blois, 13
Blunden, Edmund, 10
Bonneville, Private, 76
Boone, Captain, 81
Bordeaux, 2, 30, 76, 94
Bourbelin, 124
Bouresches, 44, 48, 49, 52, 72, 73–75, 76, 81, 94, 95, 96, 98, 109, 112–113, 128, 130
Boxer Rebellion, 26
Boyce, Major, 114
Brabson, Major, 109
Brest, 87, 106
Brest-Litovsk, Treaty of, 6
Brewster, A. W., Major General, 92
British Fifth Army, 7
Brown, Preston, Colonel, 16–18, 22, 27–28, 47, 74, 80, 96, 111, 133, 139
Bruce, Andrew, Captain, 98, 129
Bundy, General, 19, 24, 27–29, 43, 60, 61, 80, 93, 108, 110–111, 119, 121, 122, 133–135, 136, 139
Burns, Captain, 100
Bussiares, 44, 52, 96, 100, 136
Byington, Private, 132–133

Caillaux, Joseph, 2
Cambrai, 97
Cantigny, 14
Caporetto, 6, 31
Carrel, Alexis, 89
Carrel-Dakin tubes, 90
Cary, Edward, Private, 69–70
Catlin, Albertus, Colonel, 24, 25–26, 38, 39, 40–41, 43, 44, 48, 62–63, 67, 68–69, 72, 75, 136

Chamberlaine, William, Brigadier
General, 99
Chamigny, 47
Champagne, 9
Champillon (village), 59
Champillon Wood, 107
Château-Thierry, 17, 23, 24, 28,
29, 84, 93, 111–112, 135, 139
Chaumont, 1–3, 13, 60
Chaumont-en-Vexin, 16, 18–21,
123
Chemin des Dames, 12, 32, 85
Chicago *Tribune*, 51, 61, 92
Civil War, 5, 27, 88
Clemenceau, 5, 9, 10–11, 29, 31–
34, 136, 140
Clignon River, 52, 96, 101
Clumber, Private, 132–133
Code names, 42, 106, 109, 120
Cole, Edward, Major, 54, 100
Collège de Juilly, *see* Juilly
Compiègne, 3, 93
Connor, Fox, 110–111
Conta, von, General, 45, 122
Corps Conta, 45, 97, 113, 119,
121, 124, 126–127
Coupru, 28
Courcelles, 123
Crowther, Orlando, 56
Cummings, S. C., Lieutenant,
102–103

Dakin, Henry, Doctor, 89
Dakin solution, 89
Daly, Dan, Sergeant, 51, 75
Degoutte, General, 26–28, 35, 43,
47, 108, 120, 138
Denikin, General, 31
Dennis, Lieutenant, 100
de Pierrefeu, Jean, 16
Derby, Richard, Lieutenant Colo-
nel, 59–60, 80–81
Dessai, Lieutenant Commander,
59
"Devil Dog," 58
Donaghue, Robert, Sergeant, 99
Doyen, General, 25
Duchesne, General, 13, 16, 22,
23–24, 26, 28, 36, 85, 120
Dunbeck, Captain, 108
Duncan, Donald, Captain, 73–74
Dunlavy, Herbert, Private, 74

Eddy, Lieutenant, 48

Elliott, Charles, Major, 79–80,
113, 119–120, 128, 129–130
English Channel, 7, 39
Evans, Major, 38, 39–40, 71, 76,
95, 98

F Company, 95
Farwell, Major, 68, 80
Feland, Colonel, 77, 79, 133
Flame throwers, 49
Fleitz, Morris, Private, 75–76
Foch, General, 3, 8, 9, 12–13, 17,
32–35, 85, 93, 96
"Forty-or-eights," 19
Foster, Pell, 46
French Air Force, 42
French High Command, 12, 23,
34
Fuller, Captain, 100

Gandelu, 23
Garvin, Lieutenant, 57
Gas, *see* Poison gas
Gas masks, 114, 118, 119
Geary, William J., Sergeant Ma-
jor, 137
Geer, Corporal, 56
German High Command, 111, 115
Gibbons, Floyd, 51, 61–62, 64–66,
91
"Gob Gully," 47, 62, 66–67, 76,
83, 99
Gobert (ravine), 47; *see also*
"Gob Gully"
Gough, General, 7
Graves, Robert, 10
Guadalcanal, 140

H Company, 94
Hadrot, Lieutenant, 60, 61
Haig, Field Marshal, 9
Haller, Private, 76
Hamilton, George, Captain, 54–
57, 61
Hanlon Field, 117
Hanlon, Peter, Corporal, 117
Harbord, Brigadier General, 24–
26, 28, 43, 46–49, 53, 60–61,
62, 71–72, 74, 81, 93, 94, 98,
99, 101, 102, 106, 110, 111, 113,
121, 131–132, 133–136, 137, 140
Hartzell, A. E., Lieutenant, 64–66
Haxthausen, von, Major General,
97
Hebel, Private, 104

Hill 142, 53, 55, 56, 61, 120
Hill 165, 36
Hindenburg, von, 6, 7
Hoffman, Charles, Sergeant, 57
Holcomb, Thomas, Major, 48, 62, 72–74, 75, 76, 77, 79, 80, 94, 95, 96, 120
"Hook," the, 110, 113, 135
Howe, Private, 67
Hughes, John A., Major, 99–102, 105, 108–109, 112–113, 121
Hungary, 7
Hutier, von, General, 13

I Company, 99, 128
Ireland, General, 85
Irwin, Wallace, 76–77
Isle Adam, l', 19
Issonge Farm, 46
Italy, 6, 31, 128
Iwo Jima, 140

James, Edwin L., 51
Janson, Ernest, 57; see also Hoffman, Sergeant
Juilly, 83, 84, 85–91

Kahn, Otto, 94
Keyser, Ralph, Major, 134
Knights of Columbus, 129
Kolchak, Admiral, 31
Korean War, 42
Kukoski, John, Private, 55

La Loge Farm, 46, 60, 101, 134
La Voie du Chatel, 38, 58, 101, 106
"Laconia," 51–52
Lardner, Ring, 52
Larned, Reverend Doctor, 113–114
Laspierre, Tribot, Captain, 62, 68
League of Nations, 30–31
Lee, Harry, Lieutenant Colonel, 68–69, 71–72, 94
Legendre, Lieutenant, 23, 38, 39, 77–78
Leonard, H. A., Corporal, 98–99
Leonard, Wallace, Lieutenant, 74
Les Mares Farm, 36, 39
Lewis, Edward, General, 79, 80, 110–111
Limoges, 13
"Lizzie" (Ford truck), 75–76; see also Pearce, Elizabeth, Mrs.

Lloyd George, 5, 8–9, 10, 11, 32–34, 93, 140
London, 2, 30
London Agreement, 10, 11
Long, John H., Doctor, 87–89
"Lorette, The Conquerors of," 97, 113
Lucy-le-Bocage, 36, 44, 47, 49, 51, 53, 61, 62, 69, 72, 74, 76, 77, 79, 94, 95, 99, 102, 105, 109, 119
Ludendorff, 6, 7, 9, 12, 112
"Lusitania," 63, 128

Madsden, Edmund, Sergeant, 64
Malone, Paul, Colonel, 79–80, 138
Maps, lack of, 47, 48, 77, 101
March, Peyton, General, 30
Marigny, 37
Marne, 2, 17, 22, 23, 31, 122
Marshall, Ralph, Lieutenant, 66, 67
Mathis, Lieutenant, 80
May-en-Multien, 22, 23, 24, 28
McAndrew, James, General, 62
McCloskey, Colonel, 46
Meaux, 17, 18, 21, 22, 83
Mery, 132
Milner, Lord, 10–11, 29, 32
Milner, D. B., Lieutenant, 70
Milner, Drinkard, Lieutenant, 108
Montgivrault, see Montgivrault Grand; Petit Montgivrault
Montgivrault Grand, 72, 73
Montreuil-aux-Lions, 24, 36
Moore, Private, 67
Moore, William, Captain, 128–129, 130
Moore, William, Lieutenant, 75, 94

Naulin, General, 120, 122
Negro infantry, 9
Neuilly, 22
Neumann (German soldier), 126
Neville, Colonel, 36, 38, 41, 48, 62, 101
New York Times, 51, 63, 92, 111
New York Tribune, 51, 91
Noyen-Montdidier sector, 45, 96

One Man's War, 66–67
"Operation Michael," 7
Orlando, 29, 31–32, 34
Osborne, Weedon (dental surgeon), 73–74

Paris, 2, 3, 12, 17, 18, 29, 31, 33–34, 41, 69, 89, 93, 94, 119, 139, 140

Paris-Metz highway, 22, 28, 41, 46, 80

Pasfini sector, 22

Paysley, Lieutenant, 132

Pearce, Elizabeth, Mrs., 75

Pershing, General, 1–4, 6, 8–9, 10–11, 13–14, 25, 31–34, 62, 85, 93, 94, 110, 122, 139, 140; "Black Jack," 4; earlier service, 4; death of wife, 4; personality, 3–4, 25

Pétain, General, 1–3, 13–14, 23, 93

Petit Montgivrault, 80

Philippines, 4, 30, 75

Picardy, 8

Platt, Jonas, Lieutenant, 55

Poison gas, 49, 112, 114 *et seq.*, 123, 140; effects of, 115–118; first gas attack at Belleau Wood, 119; first use in war, 115; kinds of, 115–117

Poland, 7

Portuguese forces, 9

Pottle, Frederick, 90–91

Quick, John, Major, 75

Reims, 2, 12

Rendînelli, Joseph, Corporal, 66–67

Richardson, Major, 110–111

Ridgway, Matthew, General, 139

Robertson, James, Lieutenant, 73–75, 98

Robinson, Fielding S., 46

"Rosalie," *see* Bayonet, French

Roumania, 6

Rupprecht, Crown Prince, 12, 13

Russia, 6, 31, 128

Russian Front, 7, 13

St. Agon, 67

St. Aignon, 106

St. Denis, 21

Salonika, 2

Sarrail, General, 2

Sassoon, Siegfried, 10

Senegalese, 39

Serbia, 6

Shea, Richard, Lieutenant, 59–60

Shearer, Major, 107, 113, 133, 134–135, 137

Siberia, 31

Sibley, Berton, Major, 48, 62–63, 66, 67–75, 77, 82, 94, 95, 98, 99

Simpson, Roy, Private, 64

Sixth French Army, 14, 17, 120

Sleet, Private, 67

Sofsky (German soldier), 125

Soissons, 2, 12, 23, 24

Somme, 14, 17, 97

Sonnino, Baron, 29

Spanish-American War, 26, 27

Steck, F. E., Private, 103–104

Stockham, Fred, Sergeant, 120

Supreme War Council, 10–12, 29, 29–35, 94

Swink, Lieutenant, 128–129

Swiss neutrality, 12

"Syracuse" brigade, 27

Thomason, John W., Jr., Captain, 53, 58

"Throw Backs," 43

Timmerman, Louis, Lieutenant, 69

Tonkinese, 18

Torcy, 44, 47, 48, 50, 52, 53, 56, 77, 79, 100, 136, 138

Tours, 30

Triangle Farm, 94

Turkey, 31

Turrill, Julius, Major, 47, 52–54, 57, 60, 61, 62, 77, 102, 107, 108

Vera Cruz, 51, 75

Verdun, 76, 97

Versailles, 10, 29–35

Veuilly Wood, 36

Villa, Pancho, 4, 51

Villaret, Pilot-Observer, 138

Villmuth, Lieutenant, 113

Viviani, 33

Vosges, 7, 12

Waddill, Major, 79–80

Wallace, Colonel, 30

Warren, Francis (Senator), 4

Washington, 5, 33; *see also* Wilson, President

Wass, Lester, Captain, 122

Welch, William H., Doctor, 87

Western Front, 7

Weygand, General, 32

Whitney, Casper, 51, 91–92

Williams, Lloyd, Captain, 39, 77, 101, 103, 105

146

Wilson, President, 5, 6, 9, 33, 34, 94

Wilson, Sir Henry, 31

Wilson, James, General, 30

Wise, Colonel, 22–23, 36–39, 43, 58–59, 77–79, 100, 101, 102, 105–106, 107, 108–110, 111–114, 120–121, 122–123, 134

World War II, 42, 57, 116, 140

YMCA, 91, 128

Ypres, 9, 12, 115, 116

Zane, Randolph, Captain, 75, 98

Zwicky, William, Lieutenant, 124–126